FROM CHASING *to* CHOSEN

KELSEY GAUDREAULT

From Chasing to Chosen

Published by Reaching & Rooted
www.reachingandrooted.org

Edited by The Reaching & Rooted Publishing Team

ISBN: 978-1-961826-20-5 (Paperback)

Printed in United States of America

CONTENTS

DEDICATIONS

To my son, Laith.

You awoke what will forever be one of my favourite parts of life: Being a mom.

You are brave, kind, loving, wild, and fearless—everything a man needs to be a true King in this world.

The day you were born was the most beautiful day of my life. The world is better with you in it.

I will love you. Eternally and always.

My beautiful boy.

To Julio,

I wouldn't be here, with the awareness I have of myself and what it truly takes to embody sacred union, without you. These teachings came alive through us and through the making and refining of our union. For that, I will forever be grateful.

To my stepdaughters,

They say that having a son first is to learn the definition of unconditional love, and having daughters is to be taught how to become the woman they need.

Through the years I have known the three of you, I have become the type of woman I needed as a child—and the woman I was always meant to be.

Thank you for inspiring me to become the type of woman you can look up to.

ACKNOWLEDGEMENTS

To my sisters,

Thank you for seeing the depths of me and loving me exactly as I am.

Every woman needs women in her corner. I am blessed to have some of the most magical, mystical, and powerful women in mine.

I love you.

To the women who work with me,

My path as a priestess and teacher is not something I take lightly, nor something I could ever walk away from. You are what inspires me to show up, every single day. Money was never what motivated me. You are.

Thank you for allowing me to live my purpose.

FOREWORD

As we prepared to publish this book, there was a lot of talk about the deeper energetics of polarity and how they relate to humans as a whole. I think it's really important to see beyond the depths of these words and feel them vibrationally with your soul. Although I will often reference heteronormative relationships as the vast majority of the women that work with me are women searching for their husbands, this work lives far beyond the physicality of this realm. We are touching on deep universal laws. All human beings have both masculine and feminine energy within them, and we all embody different percentages of each. I can say that although I am deeply feminine, I am also very masculine. That is what allows me to run my businesses the way I do, stay consistent with my fitness, and drive forward powerfully towards my goals.

The point of this is that no matter who you are, the principles in this work can and do apply to you, regardless of your sexual orientation, the gender you identify with, and where you stand in the world.

All couples need to learn to harmonize their masculine and feminine energies to come into union, and this is what this book is about.

Use it as it works for you.

Apply it to the relational dynamic that feels true to you.

You can even apply these principles to money, your business, your social media presence, and all things in external reality, as a response to the feminine within.

Stay open, stay present, and allow this book to work through you in the way it's meant to.

I'm happy you're here.

Kelsey

INTRODUCTION

I've been a relationship coach for years, and for most of that time, I rarely talked about chasing.

Abandonment? Sure.

Emotional unavailability? Totally.

But chasing?

I never talked about it much. I'd been able to pinpoint my wounds to abandonment and emotional unavailability and not knowing how to be myself, but it wasn't until recently that I connected all of the dots to chasing. Which is wild, because "chasing" is actually something I've been doing for most of my life.

Chasing and ending the pattern of chasing has actually been at the root of my work this entire time. And the thing that led not only to the partnership, life, and business I have now, but also to my deepest spiritual awakening. It's funny how things only click and make sense when they're meant to.

Over twelve years ago, converted religions for my first marriage in an attempt to prove my worth and enoughness—though I never would have been able to admit that at the time. I genuinely believed I was making the right choice for 22 year-old me–only to have it end anyway, forcing me to face some of my deepest wounds.

My now ex-husband told me early on that he didn't think I was "the one". Rather than fully hearing and accepting that, I changed my entire identity in an attempt to prove that I was.

This is something we sometimes do to avoid facing the truth and the pain buried deep within. Not yet understanding that not being a match for someone has nothing to do with your worth or enoughness, but that's the wound it touches.

And until that wound is healed, we'll do anything and everything to avoid feeling the deep pain that it causes us within. Deep down, I knew the marriage and relationship weren't right, but to admit that would have been to face what I clearly wasn't yet ready to face.

And so I converted to Islam. I wore a hijab for three years—a part of my past that I don't love, if I'm being very honest. A part I've tried really hard to run and hide from. And that's often how you know a decision you're making might not be stemming from the right place: When there's a need to hide, it's a sign of shame.

I spent those years not seeing my dad's side of the family, again, too young and too unaware to understand the deeper unconscious layers at play within my being.

And I want to be really clear. My ex husband never pressured me to wear the hijab. However, he did make it very clear that he would not be with a woman who didn't, so I became the thing I *thought* he wanted.

This is what chasing does. It has you jumping mental hoops, looking outside yourself, *trying* to become what you *think* someone wants you to be, so they choose you.

This pattern didn't start with him, or with any man. It started with my mom. With her, the energy was always: "Do better. Okay, you got an A minus, but why didn't you get an A plus?"

And although she loved me, I spent much of my life being who *she* wanted me to be, rather than who *I* wanted to be, in an attempt to gain her love. I later chose men who I would have me feeling like I was never enough, perpetuating the same wound.

Because that's what we do, we choose the men that could never choose us to prove that we will never, in fact, be chosen.

Luckily, I went through an initiation that so many women have gone through before me: The birth of my son, and stepped into the innate wisdom and power I had never felt before. There's a lot that went into his birth. I made choices for myself. I birthed naturally, something that was deemed not okay amongst my peers at the hospital, and went against them and did it anyway. I could write an entire chapter about my birthing experience and how that night was the most beautiful night of my life.

Not only did I break free from the illusions our society has us living within—that we are incapable and unable to do something naturally that our bodies were created to do—but I also broke free from illusions I had been living in regarding who I was and what I was capable of. Giving birth, those first weeks after, and motherhood as a whole have helped me discover what a powerful, ancient goddess of a woman I am. I will forever feel blessed to be a woman for this reason. Nothing and no one can ever understand what this actually feels like, or take this away from you.

From motherhood on, everything changed.

It was the beginning of my being no longer able to live a lie. Something that only gets bigger and bigger as you continue trekking on your healing journey.

Because yes, this book is about love, but more than anything, it's about you. And as you uncover the patterns lying dormant within you, you will identify areas where you are living inauthentically in all aspects of your life.

And so I chose not to continue my career at the hospital as a respiratory therapist and started my business. Although I loved my work and missed it a lot, I knew that there was something else out there for me. At that time, I didn't quite know what it was, but I started studying for my personal training certification and making content online. I started binging podcasts and filling my brain with people living their dreams, and a truth began to awaken within me.

A truth that was always there: I wasn't meant for a normal life and a normal job and a white picket fence, although there is absolutely nothing wrong with that, but it just wasn't me. None of it was me. But to admit that all at once would be too much for our heart, soul and consciousness. And so we take these things in strides. We receive bite-sized information and take baby steps until we gain the strength to go deeper, higher and wider.

When my son was about 7 months old, I'd been following some entrepreneurs on Instagram and won tickets to a conference in San Diego. To be clear, this was a big deal. I was dying to go to her conference, so much so that I wrote it on a dry-erase board in my kitchen: "Pays to Be Brave, October 2019," and went to bed every single night imagining myself being there—prime manifesting techniques, right here, learned from Neville Goddard himself. It was truly meant to be, since I wasn't even able to enter the contest.

I remember stopping the car, filming my 1-minute application, not being able to get my video in due to some weird tech issue, and feeling, deep in my soul, that I was meant to go there. Sad and disappointed that I couldn't enter while knowing I was supposed to go, I got a random Instagram DM, and it was her. The event's owner and organizer personally gifted me a free ticket to her 3-day event in San Diego. I have chills as I write this.

Life can be so magical. It really can, because without that event, I wouldn't be here. I wouldn't. To be writing this and looking back on how everything happened and panned out exactly as it was meant to is a really surreal experience. To really know, surrender and understand that all of it, the seemingly 'good' as well as the 'bad' were all happening for you, is freedom in itself.

And so there I was, on a rooftop in San Diego, after doing an hour of breathwork for the first time in my life, while experiencing deep jaw tensions and tears streaming down my face at about 5 minutes in, hearing: "You're living a lie. There's a truth you're not sharing."

I have always been known to be bold. Just the day before, I had gone up in front of 500 women, grabbed a mic and told everyone I quit my job. I was going all in on my business, so of course, when I experienced deep jaw tension for the entire breathwork session, I walked right up and asked the teacher what she meant.

Immediately, I knew, I felt it within my soul. A truth that had been there since the very beginning. A truth I did everything to cover up from myself and everyone around me. "I'm not Muslim."

I cried the the car ride home from the airport. I knew it was over. I knew we wouldn't stay together. I knew hijab was his non-negotiable.

I kept wearing it for one more month and tried. But on my 28th birthday, on a family trip to Curacao with the support of my stepdad and his wife, I decided to take it off. And keep it off.

Overnight, I lost about 500 followers. I was sent Instagram DMs calling me a "whore", telling me "I looked uglier without it". It was a lot. I can understand that for a lot of my followers, it was confusing to be following a convert and to see her make the decision that it wasn't for her. And yet, again, just as with the birth of my son and choosing to do it naturally despite people telling me I was "stupid" and "going to die" and that my son would die (something I could never imagine telling a pregnant woman, gosh), I did something for me. The true me. And that continued to deepen my power and truth, setting off changes throughout the rest of my life.

What was devastating about my divorce was not the loss of the relationship with my ex-husband, because realistically, you can't build that much intimacy with somebody that you can't be yourself with. Although I am grateful for the lessons and for the beautiful baby we created, that was never my man. That wasn't the man I was meant to spend my life with, or would flourish with, or become the woman I was always meant to be with. What was devastating and what really was the catalyst for my most profound spiritual awakening was the loss of my family.

As a child who grew up with a single mom, I never wanted to be one. I spent my entire life wanting and dreaming of having a family. And so *this* is what put me into an intense, dark night of the soul. This was the pain that broke not only me, but the inner child within me that felt as though she had finally healed one of her deepest wounds and desires. Through this experience, I gained awareness that I unconsciously chased and chose a man who couldn't choose me to perpetuate my deep wound of feeling like no one could love me for who I was.

And it wasn't until my divorce that I realized I'd actually been doing that my entire life: Changing myself to prove my enoughness to others and be loved.

I think what I love most about the topic of chasing is that it's deep—way deeper, and more layered and intricate than at first glance.

Chasing behaviour can look one way for one woman and another entirely for another.

Yet, under the surface, within the energetic tapestries, it is the same thing.

And your girl over here, with her Sag Sun, Scorpio Mars, and 5/1 placement in Human Design, doesn't just love learning, teaching, and philosophizing…she loves to go to the deepest of depths. So that means I've studied chasing to the Nth degree.

Now, the thing with chasing is that, for adult women, it isn't as apparent as it might have been when we ran after the boys at recess.

It's more subtle—far more subtle.

It doesn't even need to look like initiating and texting first (although it could).

If you follow me on Instagram, you know the posts on chasing tend to go viral. Every. Time.

Why? Because chasing is more interesting than just who texts first.

You could be leaning back, not texting first, and still be unconsciously chasing energy.

And that means he will, inevitably, start running (we'll dive deeper into this in later chapters).

So you might be wondering, if chasing isn't as obvious as you planning dates, calling him first, or approaching him at the gym, then what is it actually?

It's you, unconsciously and somatically, contorting, performing, acting, trying, and doing to get the outcome you so deeply want to achieve.

Example: You're letting him initiate, you're letting him make the plans…but you're also checking his IG stories religiously and keeping your Saturday open just in case he wants to make plans.

It's you being attached to him choosing you—in fact, *needing* him to choose you.

And it's not that you actually want him.

It's that you *want* to be *wanted.*

You want to be chosen, because being chosen feels like proof that you matter—that you're finally enough.

Which isn't coming from purified feminine desire.

It's coming from a sense of lack deep within your being, a void that hopes his validation will finally make the emptiness/void go away.

But sadly, it won't.

Temporarily? Maybe.

But lastingly? No.

In the pages that follow, we're going to explore places within yourself that have likely been untouched for a very long time (or possibly ever). And you're going to remember the truth of who you *Are*, not who you were conditioned to be.

You'll make a vow and a commitment to live every single moment, from here on out, with the energy of knowing and embodying the frequency of being chosen.

Because that is what you deserve.

And that was how it was always meant to be.

PART I:
THE CHASE

Seeing the Pattern

Chapter 1

WHAT CHASING REALLY IS

So, if chasing isn't about texting first or planning dates…what is it actually about?

Let me be clear: Chasing can present as initiating in the ways commonly recognized. And for many of you, it does present this way, especially at the beginning of your journey of learning how to date better.

But here are some other, less obvious examples:

- Texting him after a date to tell him you had a good time, not from desire but from a fear you may have said or done the wrong thing.
- Calling him after you haven't heard from him in a few days, while feeling anxious that he hasn't texted you.
- Trying to convince him to be in a relationship with you after he's clearly told you he wasn't interested in anything serious.

But surprisingly, chasing can also present as acting unbothered, not texting him even though you really want to, and pretending to be chill.

Why? Because chasing actually has very little to do with your actions and everything to do with the energy underneath them.

Chasing energy starts with lack.

A feeling that something you need—love, validation, security—exists outside of you.

And when we feel lack, we then start to feel fear.

Fear of being abandoned.
Fear of not being chosen.
Fear that we are not enough.

From that fear comes control, performance, and strategy.

Chasing is when you step out of your natural, feminine beingness and move into a state of strategy to *get* what you want.

This is why it feels so tricky to heal. Because most women think chasing is about the physical actions you're taking.

So they try to fix the behaviour.

They stop reaching out.

Stop sharing their feelings.

Pull their energy so far back that he doesn't even know they're interested anymore… which is another problem. And yet, for some reason, he still ends up pulling away and still doesn't choose them.

Because chasing isn't about your behaviour.

It's about the reasoning behind it.

The way I want you to look at it is this:

Any time you are moving from fear that he won't like you, want you, or choose you, you are chasing.

And when we're in fear (when we don't feel safe and don't trust), we usually end up doing the one thing that gives us an illusion of safety: Taking control.

This is why being a "Black Cat" has been so popular.

(ICYMI: Black Cat was a social media trend in 2024 and 2025, encouraging women to act unbothered, taking on the qualities of a black, independent cat, to get their boyfriend, or the man they're seeing, to act like a golden retriever. Content creators shared photos of celebrities, pointing out who was a black cat and who was a golden retriever, based on posture and body language.)

The Black Cat archetype gives us an illusion of control.

An illusion of safety.

But it's laced with mechanisms of wounding, performance, and protection.

Unless you are naturally a cold, detached woman, acting like a Black Cat won't bring you closer to the man you're actually meant to be with.

It will call in other men. Men operating within surface-level versions of themselves, who would rather play games than lay down at the altar of love.

After my divorce, I totally went down the Black Cat route even before it became a trending hashtag.

It was a protection mechanism born out of my fears of love and being hurt again.

In my Black Cat era, I gained 20 pounds, kept everyone at bay, and consistently called in "emotionally unavailable" men, not realizing that I was the one completely disconnected from hundreds of parts of myself.

This left me closed-hearted and completely out of alignment with who I was truly meant to be– in literally every way.

This, by the way, is emotional unavailability—to oneself and then, by extension, also to others.

When you think about it, if you're putting on a show or in protection mechanisms and hyper-independence, you aren't surrendered.

You aren't aligned.

You're chasing safety.

Control.

Connection on your terms, which, if we're being honest, sounds a lot like the emotionally unavailable or avoidant men you keep matching up with. Right?

They want the relationship...as long as it works for them and doesn't ask too much of them.

Likewise, when you fall into performance and keep your cards close to your heart, you maintain control.

You stay in "power."

And while it may feel good in the moment. Unfortunately, it's the opposite of love.

The opposite of what you're looking for.

You don't *truly* want to protect yourself.

I mean, sure, parts of you do.

But what you really want is to be loved.

Deeply loved for all that you are...seen, adored, and cherished for the depths of you.

This can't—and won't—happen as long as you're employing strategies and holding onto illusions of control to create the perfect conditions for love to arrive.

Rather, you need to let go.

You need to re-center into your heart, your womb, and the truest aspects of you. And allow yourself to be loved.

Seen.

And...possibly...even hurt or rejected.

Because that, truly, is the only path towards real, lasting, soul-aligned love.

Chapter 2

THE WOUND BENEATH THE WANT

Okay, so I know you think you want him. And yeah, I'm sure he's great and interesting and all that. But if you and I were to dig really deep you'd probably realize that it's never actually been about him.

Sure, you have a desire for a relationship, marriage, and maybe even a family and kids. Yet, more often than not, you can't even see the man in front of you, because you are way too clouded by the wounded parts of you that are, in fact, desperate for something else...

Desperate to be seen.

To be felt.

To escape the pain inside of you that you have yet to unpack.

It's easy to chase a man.

It's easy to receive a quick hit of dopamine that takes you out of your anxious spell and finally allows you to breathe a sigh of relief, giving you the feeling that everything is going to be okay.

But it isn't.

Because underneath your response to his reassurance, his compliments, and planned dates, lies something far more insidious: A dull ache that, when you examine it, becomes an overflowing tsunami.

Unworthiness.

Shame.

Not good enough.

And everything else you've pushed under the carpet in hopes of never having to address it.

This may come as a shock to you, but you could finally call in the love of your life, spend Friday night cuddled up with him, and wake up the next morning still feeling completely unfulfilled because he and his love were never meant to fill you.

I remember when I got back with my partner after a year and a half of separation. I felt so excited, so complete, that I completely let my business fall to the wayside.

This was something I'd been working at for over five years. But instead of continuing to pursue my own dream, I would go with him to his job sites—just jumping straight into his life, as though mine was less important. I even started helping him with work for his business.

Although we were both thrilled to be back together, we weren't truly happy.

We were fighting more than I'd like to admit, neither of us realizing that I was moving further and further out of alignment with myself; further and further from the woman with whom he and I were both so deeply and utterly in love.

I remember one evening about seven months into our rekindled relationship, I sat on our bed in the house we'd just moved into together, and cried. He stood there in front of me and asked me where I'd gone. It hit me: The me we both knew was the me in my mission, my purpose, and my business.

I quickly got back in the saddle, spent four weeks posting consistently online, created the framework for my now-signature program UNION, launched it, and finally started to feel like me again.

Your man is not you.

Sure, he can be a reflection of you, but no matter how much he loves you or cares about you, he will never be able to fill the gaping hole within you that was only ever meant to be filled with your Self (your goals, dreams, purpose) and the love of God.

And when we are chasing a man, what we are really doing is avoiding…

Ourselves.

Our dreams and desires.

Our power and all that we are meant for.

It's easier to obsess over what he meant by that text than it is to sit with your own bigness...

Easier to try and analyze his behaviour than to finally write the book...

Easier to chase him than show up for yourself.

Because when you do finally show up for you, everything you've been avoiding comes up to the surface:

The doubt, the unconscious, buried negative beliefs, the parts of you that don't know if you're actually worthy of the life you say you want.

And so the chase becomes a distraction.

A sneaky coping mechanism.

A way to temporarily relieve the discomfort of your own becoming.

But at the root, it's all the same thing, really.

You chase him so that you can feel good enough. Because to sit with yourself, to truly be with yourself and write the book or create the content or go for the career you actually want, stirs up the feelings you don't want to feel...the ones that have always been there.

Chasing the man is a distraction.

Now, is your man, the man who's meant for you, a distraction? Absolutely not. But are you using him as a distraction and a band-aid to cover up what you've been unwilling to face within yourself?

Probably.

Signs you're using him as a distraction or band-aid:

- You only feel calm or confident when he's texting you, giving you attention, or actively pouring into you.
- You're more excited by the idea of a relationship than by the actual man standing in front of you.
- You abandon your dreams, goals, and sense of self the moment a man enters the picture.
- Being chosen by him feels more important than choosing yourself.

It sucks.

And it's hard to recognize.

I know, because I've been there.

Even as I write this book, I am here, in it with you, feeling all the beliefs and reasons why I've been unwilling to do this until now.

Thirty minutes before writing this, I was randomly flooded with a memory of the child-on-child sexual abuse I experienced as a little girl.

A memory I had, for years, and thought nothing of—only to realize it was at the literal root of all of my issues, all of my sabotage, all of my avoidance.

An experience that rocked me so deeply to the core that I felt as unworthy as anyone could ever feel.

An experience that had me push away love anytime it got close, as I felt I deserved nothing more than degradation and tiny fractions of love.

An experience that has kept me from truly embodying and becoming the woman I was created to be, until now.

It's hard.

I know.

So now that we've established what chasing is, what does *Real Love* feel like, in contrast?

It's likely going to be different for everyone, and it can be really confusing when you're actively healing, but from what I've seen and known, it has nothing to do with butterflies.

(The butterflies are actually more likely a sign you're walking down a deep, dark, karmic path, riddled with unconscious tendencies attempting to close out old trauma loops.)

Real love has nothing to do with how much he texts or doesn't text and everything to do with who he *Is*.

And whether or not you can see, feel, and love him at his core—not for what he can do, but for his depth, heart, and soul.

Real love wants to meet you in the space between two whole humans who are no longer hiding, shrinking, or self-abandoning in an attempt to be chosen—two humans in their enoughness and power, ready to stand unwavering in the face of love.

And until you reach this point, you will continue to confuse the chase with connection.

Underneath the chase—underneath the wanting and yearning and grabbing for his love and attention—is a far deeper part of you, yearning, wanting, and grabbing for your *own* love and attention.

This part of you yearns for you to finally see her, be with her, and know her.

The only way to break the pattern of chasing is to become really clear on what it is you're chasing, what it is you're really wanting, and where it's coming from.

What unmet needs are still alive in your body?

What abandonment wounds are yet to be processed?

Which stories have you been telling yourself that are finally ready to be cleared and let go of?

Chapter 3

PERFORMANCE DISGUISED AS POWER

Feminine power is different from masculine power. That's one of the reasons why it felt so confusing. When we look at a man, what makes him powerful?

His strength? Status? Ability to lead, provide, protect, etc.

These are qualities our society loves, wants more of, and rewards. But these expressions of power are masculine, not feminine.

I don't know about you, but growing up, even though I was an artist and loved drama, drawing, and reading, my parents pushed academics. I wanted nothing more than to be an actress and model, but those dreams were seen as unrealistic and…frivolous? Silly?

Unimportant. Starving artist vibes.

What was supported? Cadets. Good grades. College to become a respiratory therapist, aka a "real" career.

Not to mention, the boys at school rarely give a girl attention for her sense of style, makeup, or the way she does her hair. More often, they laugh and poke fun at her, but when she meets them on the soccer field, they notice and respect her.

But growing up, I was not a sports girl in any way, shape, or form. A runner? Sure. Weightlifter? 100%. That's the OG love of my life. But sports? No. I'd rather sit on the sidelines reading *The Vampire Chronicles* (which, obviously, wasn't "cool", either).

I used to have this thing where I would watch zombie shows. I was obsessed with *The Walking Dead*. Excluding vampires, my lifelong obsession, I'd only let myself watch darker, more masculine shows. Five or six years ago, before I started on this feminine path, I didn't let myself love shows like Bridgerton or anything else feminine in that way. I wouldn't let myself be the feminine version of myself.

I remember hearing in a podcast: "A lot of girls weren't admired and loved by the boys unless they were one of the boys."

It hit me. Thinking back to school, I remember that the guys might think you're hot, but realistically, I feel like the boys love you when you're one of the boys. At least, that was the experience I had growing up.

When you're one of the boys, when you're playing out in the field with them, when you're gaming with them, then they want to talk to you. But if you want to talk to them about Kim Kardashian, they're not interested, right?

I feel like a lot of us just become more masculinized. I used to play video games a lot. I feel like I completely repressed my femininity because it wasn't valued.

I do have one memory in grade four, where the boy I liked laughed at girls who wore training bras. I remember feeling completely ashamed because I had a training bra in grade four. If I didn't wear a training bra, you would have seen little pepperoni nipples in my t-shirt. Super embarrassing!

Even in high school, guys wouldn't talk to girls about this kind of thing. Even now, most of the time. I was telling my man that I'm going to become best friends with Kim Kardashian. He doesn't get it. When we're younger, we do want to be liked by the guys. We do want them to pay attention to us. We do want to talk to them. And they would only talk to us when we're doing boy stuff.

In my experience, you needed to go out in the woods and be rough and tough with them. Ride the four-wheelers, go out in the mud, because they won't respect you if you play with Barbies.

Feminine women don't want respect. We want to be cherished. But in high school, with the maturity of men, for the most part, the guys weren't cherishing you.

And so, slowly begins the conditioning into masculine qualities and out of our truest feminine nature.

When you spend so long being told you're too sensitive, too emotional, and that there's only one way to succeed in this society, you start to adopt these qualities.

You start to feel less than. Disempowered. Confused. While wanting to feel good, powerful, and worthy—and ultimately start looking for power in the same way: By achieving, controlling, succeeding. This is what happens to so many of us.

And so, we began to disconnect from our feminine.

We stopped trusting our softness, our emotions, our intuition.

We learned to chase power, the only way we saw it being respected: Through masculine traits.

We got stronger, went to the gym, and built our businesses.

We made money, became independent, and checked all the boxes we so deeply wanted a man to check.

Deep down, we didn't feel whole.

We didn't feel chosen.

And we couldn't receive real love.

Feminine power doesn't come from control.

It comes from alignment.

Truth.

Embodiment.

Now, understand this: Making money and having a business don't automatically make you masculine, just as being a homemaker doesn't automatically make you feminine.

However, many women these days have (for a variety of reasons) concluded that they need or want to be more "feminine". And unfortunately, a lot of you have, in the name of femininity, actually dropped the things that bring you life and fulfillment, only to trade them for a sneaky variation of the same thing:

- Acting unbothered.
- Black cat energy.
- Pretending not to care.
- Minimizing your truth.
- Controlling the outcome without looking like you are.

All new disguises of control.

All performances. Not power.

And obviously, none of this performance is conscious.

It's not that you're trying to be fake.

It's that you don't feel safe being real.

The black cat energy.

The pretending not to care.

The hyper-independence.

The "I'm fine."

And the cool girl who acts as if nothing bothers her.

This isn't power in any way, shape, or form.

It is, in fact, the opposite:

It's you feeling so disempowered that you have no choice but to go into protection.

Because to admit you do care…

To admit you do like him…

To admit you do, in fact, want love…

Would mean facing the possibility that he might not feel the same.

That you might be rejected.

That, despite all of your efforts, he might not want you.

And that? Well, that's scary.

Really scary.

Because to perform and not be wanted means nothing. You have a scapegoat. Something to blame. You can always say, "Well, it's not as if he even really knew me."

There's no real risk of rejection.

But to be yourself—to let down the walls, to drop the masks and the charades—and to be rejected is to hit your deepest wounds.

"What if I'm not good enough?"

"What if I'm not worthy?"

And that's what sends us into a cascade of pain. It's also what we're avoiding with this false sense of control and power.

Except, the problem is, there's no real love in control masked as power.

And to continue to believe so is to keep playing cat and mouse with men who are playing the same games (which I'm assuming you're sick of, otherwise you wouldn't be reading this book).

Yes, babe. That avoidant man you like so much is in the same patterns of control. And to stop attracting this, you need to first heal it within yourself.

Okay, now let's just clarify something else: Not all ambition is a mask.

Some of you are deeply fulfilled by your mission.

I know I am, and no polarity teaching or anything anyone says could make me say that my drive, ambition, and desire to self-actualize aren't real (because that wouldn't be true) In fact, those aspects of me are probably some of the realest things about me.

Some of you are meant to lead, to build, to do big, scary, incredible things.

Your discipline, drive, and devotion aren't masculine. They are just *you.*

At the end of the day, when we get to the bare bones of polarity and find internal union, you realize that you are both.

Masculine and feminine, together, working for the good of all that is your soul, heart, life, and mission.

Your heaven on earth.

All things in the universe have both masculine and feminine energy. Even in plants, we see both a masculine and a feminine pole at work in creating new life. Instead of viewing reality creation through the lens of manifestation, I see it through the lens of polarity. The feminine and the masculine. The feminine could be seen as the unconscious mind, with the masculine as the conscious mind. The conscious mind plants the seed, and the unconscious mind then becomes "pregnant" and brings it to life.

Even with artificial insemination, there's still a masculine seed and a female body that receives it. Together, they create life.

The feminine is receptive and magnetic. The masculine is penetrative, disciplined, decisive, and electric. The masculine carries electric potential. The feminine holds magnetic power. Together, they function like a battery.

Beyond physically, in any type of relationship, we need this battery to work properly. The masculine gives and pours into the feminine. The feminine then receives fully, expands her capacity for receptivity, allows it to change her, amplifies what she was given and then asks for more. Her desire for more invites him to become more, and the cycle continues as they both evolve in tandem.

A simplified example of this would be a woman who wants a bigger home and the man who provides that for her. In almost any relationship dynamic, there will be one who provides and one who multiplies. The feminine wants more because she's meant to birth more, and through her wanting more, the masculine becomes more.

It's a perfect system. The feminine and masculine constantly help each other elevate, ascend, and become more together. It's beautiful. These are the deeper energies. This happens internally within ourselves. Our internal feminine desires more, wants more, receives more, and then our inner masculine steps up and writes the book, starts the business, gets a better job, and then our feminine expands in her capacity. She expands her worthiness. It's like she opens her womb more to receive. This is happening at both the conscious and unconscious levels.

The conscious mind sets new goals, impregnating the unconscious, and the unconscious mind then creates the dream life. It ties into everything. I do not doubt that human beings, two-souled, non-binary, all these things, if they were to really examine, they still can feel this going on internally within themselves. I would say I haven't personally sat and reflected on the dynamics when we are outside our matching physicality, however these energies still exist internally.

But for me, I'm a woman, I know what it is to receive. I also know what it is to penetrate, as the feminine does penetrate the world with her expression, style, essence and beingness. I can't speak to someone who is a man and learning to receive, but I'm assuming it's the same thing. I've had a lot of queer female couples work with me, but no queer male couples, yet. So I don't have any experience with that.

These dynamics show up in every kind of relationship. Both want to be cherished, to be loved. But then we see the same dynamics that two powerhouse couples go through.

My stepdad and my mom had these really close friends who, when they got together, my mom and the husband would be wedding planning, and my stepdad and the wife would be watching football in the living room.

This is what I mean, there's no right or wrong. You have to find your own energetic makeup. And then let others find their own energetic makeup, let people be themselves, especially you.

One of the really big issues in polarity that my man and I had was that I was constantly trying to make him more "masculine", as though this CEO, plane flying, adventurous, jujitsu competing man wasn't already masculine so I could be more feminine. He asked me, "Can you just be the one that I fell in love with? That sales, powerful, girlboss?" Okay. I was trying to force us both into a mold that wasn't ours. Not relationally, nor personally.

So if this is you, great.

However, even if this is you, some of this masculine potential might—just might—be laced with the wounding I'm going to describe below.

For some, these traits are a coping mechanism, a way to control how you're seen.

The drive to build something, at its root, actually has nothing to do with building anything, and everything to do with proving how good you are, how strong you are, how capable, worthy, and deserving you are—to Mom, Dad, the world, etc.

But more importantly, it has everything to do with proving all of this to yourself. Because somewhere, deep down, without all this doing and all these accolades and all this success, you still don't know you are enough.

And the reality is, only *you* know the difference.

Is your drive and ambition Self-sourced? Or is it a mask you're wearing to hide the truth of what it is you currently believe to be true about yourself?

Real feminine power is vulnerable.

It is you, stripped of all you wear, all you've done.

It's you at the end of the day, crown and jewels off.

Naked.

Knowing that you are worthy and enough.

Exactly as you are.

Exactly as you have always been.

That's power.

And that's where your man wants to meet you.

JOURNAL PROMPTS

1. Be honest and ask yourself, "Why is it that I do what I do?" The first answer is always the answer. If something like "to make my parents happy" or "to prove that I'm enough" comes up, then this reveals a lot.

2. If you were alone in the world, validation and money didn't matter, would you still be doing the work you're doing?

3. Connect with your heart, inner feminine, and inner child. What type of life would bring her the most fulfillment? Is your current life in alignment with this, or does something need to change?

4. If you were to stop needing to prove your worth or enough-ness through your doing, what would you stop doing immediately?

5. What would you do and who would you be if you finally felt like you had permission to be yourself?

Chapter 4

WHY HE PULLS AWAY

This chapter isn't about the typical pulling away that happens when a man starts to get closer to you. It's about the pulling away that mirrors deeper issues within yourself.

But first, let's briefly touch on the typical one. Here's the truth: Every man is, at some point, going to pull away. He's going to take up space. This is biological. It's natural and hormonal. Men and testosterone do not mix well with deep intimacy at all times.

A man is meant to be able to go off to work. To build his business, make sales, and do the things you and he both need him to do. And if he's snuggled up with you all day, ordering Uber Eats and watching Netflix, that's not going to work. Not for him, nor for you, nor for the passionate, polarizing relationship I know you really want. It's like that whole man cave thing. Men naturally need space.[1]

But this chapter isn't about this phenomenon. It's about you noticing a pattern in yourself, about you getting closer to a man, feeling like things are *finally* going to kick off, and then *boom,* he pulls away. Ghosted. Disappeared. No longer interested. And sadly, it's something that has happened so many times before that you now have

[1] Andie Thueson, "Why Men Need Space, Something You Need to Understand," Andie Thueson - Success Starts With Soul Purpose, September 25, 2025, https://andiethueson.com/why-men-need-space/.

a deeply embedded fear that expressing your feelings, showing a man interest or opening your heart is the cause of him losing interest.

So what gives? Are women never supposed to show interest? Are you supposed to stay cold and close-hearted? Or is something else at play? Let's give you the answers you've been needing so we can finally nip this pattern in the bud once and for all.

Okay, here goes...

The masculine is a master at feeling energy. I am literally hearing you scoff and seeing you roll your eyes, because I understand this probably isn't the experience you've had, but it's true, nonetheless. Men can feel when you have walls around your heart that are never going to let them in.

As a side note, this isn't some "woo woo" fluff. It's scientific. The heart emits an electromagnetic frequency that produces a vibration six feet away.[2] This is why a guy could see you out at the grocery store, be really interested, move closer to you, and realize there is no way in hell that he is going to be able to penetrate the intense walls, vast moat, and complex traps you've laid out for him.

They can feel our energy. They can feel our wounds before we can. And here's a pro tip: Don't go asking a man in your life about this, because he won't know. He won't be able to verbalize what's happening here. He will just know he's interested in one woman, and he's no longer interested in another, and won't even be able to tell you why, because it's unconscious. Primal. Subtle energetic patterns he's feeling into.

So when you come into a dynamic with a man and you are unconsciously chasing, performing, have unmet inner childhood wounds and deep trauma that has not yet been closed out and processed (parts of you that need saving, that want to be seen, that need him to choose you to feel worthy enough, chosen, deserving, or that you matter)...

---

2 Jessica Morales, "The Heart's Electromagnetic Field Is Your Superpower," Psychology Today, November 29, 2020, https://www.psychologytoday.com/us/blog/building-the-habit-of-hero/202011/the-hearts-electromagnetic-field-is-your-superpower?msockid=0e6a70b6f3f46689275f6344f2e66762.

He can feel this. Can feel the immense pressure that your tiny little inner girl is putting on him. And runs the other way.

This is the most common reason why he pulls away.

And it sucks.

Because every time you're in a dynamic and this happens, you reaffirm all of the deep-seated beliefs that are the reason why he moves away from you. Do you see the conundrum we're in? Truly, a challenging space to navigate.

Because again, these little, wounded parts believe they're not worthy, not lovable, not enough, etc. And want a man to come in and finally make them feel like everything is okay and will finally be okay.

But on the flip side, these parts will ultimately:

A) Not actually believe anything other than what they believe to be true.

If, deep down, you don't feel worthy, a man can come in with flowers, commitment, consistency, and love, and you won't be able to receive it fully. Why?

Because it doesn't match your current paradigm, your unconscious mind needs to be morally right. So if it believes that you are not worthy, it will do everything in its power to prove that you are, in fact, "not worthy."

B) This isn't his responsibility to heal. It's yours. And he can feel the weight of it, and will more than likely resist something that was never meant to be his to hold.

C) The masculine cannot give you what you haven't yet given yourself.

We'll unpack this in future chapters, so I won't go too deep here, but it basically ties into this. We're going to go a layer deeper. We're looking at it from a different level.

I wrote an Instagram post on this, which has received over 300,000 views. Clearly, it hit a nerve.

And it stated: He is not half in—you are.

Remember how, at the beginning of this book, we talked about the very deep wounds of chasing, performing, and needing him to choose you to be loved. And these parts are ultimately more committed to getting him and being chosen than they are to your deepest self—to your truth.

So when we actually look at these parts that are looking outward to the man to choose them, what they're really doing is abandoning you. Right? They're performing for approval over being authentically you. They're trying to prove their worth instead of owning their inherent worth. They are not in alignment with you. They are not committed to you. They are not all-in with you. They do not value you. They do not see you.

These parts want something outside of themselves because something has taught them that your *own* love, God's love, your fulfillment, depth, heart, soul and entire being at large is not enough. And would rather believe that this random man from a dating app, whom you're talking to on a Tuesday night, is somehow more important than you. And could somehow actually give you more than you.

So, in actuality, you left first. He just followed.

And this is why he pulls away from you. Because you are pulling away from yourself. You are choosing him *above* yourself, and has no choice but to choose something (or someone) else over you.

So if you're wondering why he pulled away…

ask yourself: Where did I abandon myself first?

How do we break this pattern? We take our healing seriously. You stop looking to the external world and an external source of love to give you what you already have within.

You're probably thinking: "Duh, Kelsey, that's why I'm here. This is why I've been in therapy. This is why I've done Ayahuasca. This is why I do *all* the things."

I know. I get it. I hear you.

And this book is going to be a massive stride in your healing because of how deep we go.

Because at the end of the day, talking things out doesn't fully change things.

Healing on an unconscious level does.

Shifting your paradigm does.

Having a change in perspective does.

Embodying something new does.

And that's what we're gonna keep doing.

Chapter 5

THE MASCULINE MIRROR

Our unconscious mind speaks in pictures, symbols, and metaphors, which is why movies, stories, song lyrics, visual art, and books affect us so deeply.[3] We personify everything, pull meaning from them and apply that meaning to our own lives.

If you're new to the world of energetics (and new to my work), it goes something like this:

Our external reality reflects what's going on internally.

AKA: As within, so without. As above, so below.

Now, it is my belief (as many others before me have also believed) that you and your body are the entire universe at large.

The entire physical world is ultimately you, pushed out. To think we are separate from the external world is to live in an illusion.

There is no separation.

---

3 Abigail Brenner, "The Inner Language of the Subconscious," Psychology Today, January 29, 2013, https://www.psychologytoday.com/us/blog/in-flux/201301/the-inner-language-of-the-subconscious.

This falls under the law of Divine Oneness.[4]

You aren't separate from your external masculine.

You aren't separate from your dream life.

You aren't separate from anything you are meant to experience.

You might not be in alignment with some of these things…yet, but you are not separate from them.

And so, when you look at yourself and the world you live in, you need to understand that not only are you "manifesting," but you are actually birthing it and, in union with it, all while simultaneously experiencing it.

Everything is you—inside, outside, and all around you.

It's all you.

This means that when you change, the world around you changes.

And that is the crux of the work I do with my clients—the foundations of which I'm sharing with you here in this book. The goal is to shift your perception of your life, yourself, and the world at large because, as Anaïs Nin says, "We do not see things as they are, we see them as we are." [5]

And so, the external reality is always giving us data.

We live within a feedback loop of what we believe to be true about ourselves and the world we are living in.

For example…

---

[4] Flannery Dziedzic, "The Law of Divine Oneness," Medium, May 11, 2020, https://medium.com/@FlanneryDz/the-law-of-divine-oneness-b160e2f5d64.

[5] Anaïs Nin, *Seduction of the Minotaur*. (United States: Swallow Press, 1961), 124.

If a woman feels unworthy, she will—with her unconscious mind, aka the supercomputer in her mind—scan the dating apps or scan the social event she's attending and choose the man who's going to mirror back what she believes to be true about herself.

Why?

Because the unconscious mind needs to be right, it's part of its operation manual.

If you don't feel worthy and look in a worthy mirror, you won't be able to receive that information because it doesn't feel true.

Hence the importance of healing both your unconscious mind and your nervous system—in the realm of love, relationships, and ultimately all things in life (money, for example, is often a big one).

So the masculine mirrors us as he belongs to the external world, and he mirrors us in two ways:

1. In our beliefs about ourselves
2. And at times, within our own inner masculine

Now, I need you to understand a couple of things before we dive in:

Not every man is your mirror, nor is he supposed to be.

You could meet a man who is very clearly in a lower vibrational state—not at a level or standard you desire, and that means absolutely nothing about you.

There is organic consciousness, which could be seen as God, source creation energy, or Eros, the life force energy. It's the energy flowing within and through all of us. It's truth. It's real. It's raw. Alive.

Then there is the ego. The ego can be seen as a set of wounds. It is the parts of us that don't feel good enough or worthy. It isn't true. It's not connected to or rooted in God. There's not a tree or a plant in this entire universe that's asking itself if it's enough. It *knows* it's enough. It knows it's worthy. It's only human beings that create egoic subpersonalities that stem from trauma and illusion.

This entire physical reality is an illusion that we're living in. Although the trauma is real and feels very real, it's stemming from this false reality, from this illusory reality. The part of you that doesn't feel good enough is not of God. It's not of Eros. There's no life in it. They say that a body without Christ is like a carcass on the ground with animals feeding off of it. These wounded parts of ourselves are empty, and they are in service to the ego. Which means these parts are anti-life. There is no liveliness here. Only death. The part of you that doesn't feel worthy is not in service to your highest timeline, the life within, or all that you're meant to birth and experience.

She's not in service to the book that you're meant to write. Or to the babies you're meant to have, or the trek you're meant to climb at Mount Kilimanjaro, or the dream body you want to have this summer. She's in service to feeling unworthy. To holding herself back, to playing small, to sabotaging her gym routine and diet, to staying with a man with a mattress on the floor that can't even take her out for a $20 dinner. As I said: Anti-life. Anti-joy. Anti-fulfillment. Anti you being loved and adored like the radiant goddess that you are while eating steak dinner, an extra side of grilled shrimp, post your 4th glute-focused workout day of the week.

The above is what life is all about. To live as the highest expression of you. To live, trapped in the unconscious tendencies of your wounds and ego, is not only to live as a lower aspect of you but to live in a lower timeline than that which you were meant to experience.

We all have a lower energy and a higher self, or as I like to say, a false self and a true Self. All atoms are vibrating, and different energies; the ego, wounds, parts that don't feel good enough, sit lower on the scales of consciousness than states of worthiness, joy, love, curiosity, play, etc. If a man is in a lower vibrational state, he is living as his false self and operating as an egoic, wounded, smaller, less infinite version of himself.

You are consistently going to meet and attract all sorts of people. Just because you work with the healing principles in this book doesn't mean you won't encounter man-children or narcissistic men.

It just means you no longer need anything mirrored back through them.

Why would someone NEED something to be mirrored back to them by another person in this way?

Neville Goddard taught that our divine consciousness separated itself to see itself, know itself, and heal itself. You can't see yourself clearly in a fishbowl. You see yourself through other human beings. This is the only way to heal and to bring.

While Carl Jung believed the entire process of self-actualization is to bring the unconscious to consciousness, that's the entire process of self-actualization, and ultimately, being human is to bring the unconscious to conscious. It's through human beings, our interactions, the mirroring, perceptions, projections, you name it. This is how we can know ourselves more deeply. We are filled with projections, protection mechanisms that prevent us from actually knowing ourselves better and deeper.

We protect the ego that prevents us from seeing the truth of ourselves. This is why you might choose a man to reflect these things, and why you wouldn't choose a narcissist. Because that's not a clear mirror, that's not a healed mirror. That's not going to help you. If anything, that's going to hurt you. You wouldn't choose a man who makes you feel unworthy.

If you heal the part of you that didn't feel worthy, you will no longer need this man in your reality, and he will take himself out. This is why we don't chase. If part of you feels unworthy, you are a perfect puzzle piece for a man who's going to treat you less than you deserve. He aligns with what your unconscious mind believes to be true about you. Your unconscious mind needs to be morally right.

If you believe that you're unworthy, I could tell you that you're worthy, and you won't hear anything. It's in one ear and out the other because you don't believe it to be true. I'm sure you've seen this in your own healing. This is why women end up in the same patterns over and over because they haven't healed the root of what they believe to be true.

Where it starts to mean something…is where you entertain it.

Where you allow it.

Where you fall into it.

So, for example, if you meet a man who asks you to Netflix and chill and you agree, then this relationship/dynamic is showing me something you must believe to be true about yourself.

That could be that you feel unworthy of more.

Or undeserving.

Or not good enough for a man to actually take you out on a date.

I've had clients who actually had to open themselves up to a man paying for their coffee because even that felt quite far from what they were used to.

And that's okay.

Because over time, you heal and your capacity to take on more expands.

So ultimately, the man in your life (or the men you're going on dates with and entertaining) is showing you parts of yourself that are still alive and need healing and attention.

Otherwise, you would not be entertaining his BS, to put it simply.

Is this making sense?

I know it can feel a little abstract, but ultimately, as Carolyn Elliott says in *Existential Kink*, "Having is evidence of wanting." [6]

And nothing has ever felt truer than that.

Yes, that's hard to hear, because it means that somewhere, deep down, whatever you are experiencing is something you must unconsciously be wanting.

Not because you actually want it, but because in some weird way, it proves what you believe to be true about yourself.

---

[6] Carolyn Elliott, *Existential Kink: Unmask Your Shadow and Embrace Your Power* (Newburyport, MA: Weiser Books, 2020).

And although it sucks, and you wish it weren't like this, it's also giving you the key to your ultimate freedom.

I mean, how freeing is it to look at your life and relationships…

Realize that you have been birthing/creating this all along…

And now have the power to actually change something about it?

Another super interesting pattern I've seen in myself and my clients is mirroring of what's happening in your *own* inner masculine energy.

If you're new to polarity, it goes like this:

Every man and woman has both an inner masculine and an inner feminine energy.

And every one of us needs to do the work internally to heal, rise, and find internal union, which, more often than not, leads to external union with your external person.

Something I've witnessed: If you consistently match up with certain types of men with certain traits, i.e., being undisciplined, out of their power, in people-pleasing tendencies, etc., they could be trying to show you what's going on within your own internal masculine energy.

Maybe you're always fawning.

Or not showing up for spin class.

Or never following through on your own word.

You can't really expect to date someone with qualities you haven't actually embodied.

So, believe it or not, on the path to being more feminine, you do, in fact, need to become more masculine:

- Boundaried
- Disciplined
- Decisive
- Protective
- Strong

Only with a solid inner masculine can you finally soften into your feminine.

Make sense?

Let's dive into some journal prompts so you can find more awareness within yourself:

JOURNAL PROMPTS

1. What is the man in my life (or the men I'm dating) showing me that I must believe to be true about myself (e.g., that I feel unworthy, etc.)?

2. What is my life showing me that I believe to be true about myself?

3. Are the men around me mirroring qualities I need to work on within my own masculine energy? If so, what do I need to work on?

PART II:
THE COLLAPSE OF THE FALSE FEMININE

Reclaiming Your Feminine Power and Finding Internal Union

This section is, by far, my favourite part of the book. I mean, obviously, I am in love with the totality of it, but collapsing what isn't you, has never been you, and was never meant to be you is something I love to see.

I love to see you let go of all ways in which you are not yet in the absolute fullness of your deep, sacred, wild, *true* feminine power.

Something that, oddly enough, as we're talking about feminine embodiment, can only really happen once you heal, build, restore and bring your inner masculine fully online.

Something that I also feel is deeply neglected in love and dating in the online space.

You've likely consumed content telling you that you need to have better boundaries.

Higher standards.

To say "no".

With very little instruction on how you're actually meant to do that while staying "soft", "feminine", and "high value".

And it's because the key is your inner masculine.

Yes, he's *actually* needed.

The masculine, internally and externally, is needed.

And meant to be respected, appreciated, valued and trusted, and it starts with your *own* relationship with your masculine and how he shows up for you.

Which inevitably requires work on both ends—within your feminine and your masculine.

You need an inner father that is not only emotionally available, aka open to you and your soft, feminine heart, but attuned and deeply aligned with cherishing and protecting you - which happens as you begin to heal the layers of your emotional unavailability (something we'll discuss in the chapters to come.

And you need an inner feminine that finally feels safe enough to stand down, to no longer need to protect and defend yourself with wounded parts of yourself and allow your inner masculine to stand up in truth for you. Along with a deep sense of worth—knowing that you are worthy of such treatment and cherishment. Something you may have yet to feel or experience from your own father or the men in your life.

This process, of both softening and strengthening in a multitude of ways, happens simultaneously as you do this work.

And so, the entire second part of this book is dedicated to you rising, not collapsing.

And by collapsing, I mean wavering.

Settling.

Faltering.

In what it is that you know you want, but more importantly, what you need and what it is you know you deserve.

I love love.

And I'm excited for you to experience the love you deserve.

But to experience internal union.

To stay open-hearted, for possibly the first time in your life, knowing that you can trust yourself, have your back, and know that you would never abandon yourself in the face of anything, ever again, is a feeling unlike anything else.

To no longer need something outside of you and, moment by moment, stay centred, rooted and aligned with the woman that you *Are*, regardless of how someone else is showing up or not, is to be truly in your power.

To be truly free.

And although I know you want love, what you really want is to stop chasing, stop collapsing, stop pretending, and to finally just be you through and through.

Chapter 6

OVERGIVING IS NOT LOVE

Overgiving isn't love.Let me repeat it:That is NOT love.

When you are overgiving, you are not giving from overflow. You are taking from your higher self, your capital S Self, your truest Self, your feminine Self—the Self within the self.

And that means you are taking from your inner world to get something from the external world. But the external world is literally just an illusion, so how can you possibly get anything tangible from it?

I want you to imagine that overgiving is the equivalent of reaching into your body, into your heart, taking what's most cherished and precious from within you, and throwing it at a mirror that could never possibly pour into you in the way that God, life, your own inner fulfillment, and that ever-flowing, overflowing Source inside of you could.

Now that we've established that, let's talk about where overgiving comes from.

Of course, nobody is just out here thinking to themselves, "I want to overgive today." Sure, you might be thinking, "I want to give. I want to serve in my mission, in my work. I want to love my children. I want to love my man."

But no one is walking around thinking, "I want to overgive." Think of the energy of that word: Overgive. Look at what it implies, just on its face.

Over. It means you're doing too much. You're not just giving. You're taking it one step further: *Over*-giving.

Why?

Ask yourself this right now: Why do I overgive? The first answer is generally the most unconscious and the truest. Don't question it. Don't say, "I didn't have time to think."

No, you're not supposed to have time to think. That's the point. When we're working in the realm of the unconscious mind, the first answer is the answer.

So, why do you overgive?

I've been doing this a long time, sister. So I can tell you why the majority of women overgive: They don't feel good enough. They don't feel worthy. They don't feel deserving. They think they need to work hard for love. They believe they have to prove themselves to be loved. They think they have to sacrifice for love.

Does this sound like something you might be doing?

I think the most challenging part about overgiving—how do I put this without upsetting someone…not that I care to censor myself, but I love you, dear reader, and I don't want to upset you…

Here goes: Overgiving is also...a form of manipulation.

Because a lot of the time when we're overgiving, it's not coming from a true place, meaning it's not from the capital-S Self. The Self within the small self, that overflowing source of life. That kind of giving is loving. We want to give. We want to love.

Think of any children in your life. You love them.

Think of your business. I don't know about you, but my business is such a place of devotion and service for me. I want to give to my business. And the place that I'm giving from? It feels as though it never empties.

I wake up in the morning inspired, energized, ready to give from this place of wholeness and fullness. It's amazing. And when we give from this place of wholeness and fullness, we are replenished over and over and over.

Overgiving, on the other hand, isn't stemming from that place of wholeness and fullness.

It's stemming from ego.

And when you "give" from ego, you give from nothingness. From lack, which only brings more lack. This isn't the kind of giving that brings you closer to what you want — giving from your highest Self, from that overflowing source within you. That kind of giving fills you. Overgiving depletes you. It takes from you.

By ego, I don't mean a huffed-up, "I am the best, I'm the shit" energy. I mean the opposite of God, the opposite of life.

Ego is anything and everything artificial.

And ultimately, ego exposes the wounded parts of you that are empty, stemming from nothingness, and not connected to the eternal source of life.

God, the Self, the truest and highest parts of you—these are what you are deeply connected to. They are what we could call being Self-sourced. They're sourced in that life force, Eros, overflowing, abundant energy within you.

The wounded parts of you, on the other hand, are sourced from nothingness. Therefore, they're not actually real.

Maybe you're thinking, "Kelsey, my trauma is very real."

Yes, it is. You're right. But those little wounded parts that came from all that trauma? They're not organic, true consciousness. They are ego. They are egoic sub-personalities. Wounded aspects of yourself, and they're not connected to life.

They are anti-life.

So now that's established, let's rewind to the overgiving issue.

When you are overgiving, you are sourcing, or taking, from the wounded parts of you. This means you are attempting to take something out of nothingness, i.e., from lack. And you are therefore moving from a state of lack.

And oftentimes, when we overgive, it's not from a genuine place of love, desire, and connection. It's from a place of: "If I give to you...Will you love me?"

"If I do the dishes for you...Will you do the dishes for me?"

I see this happening all the time with clients, and they sound resentful and angry, saying things like, "I do the ironing, and I do the cleaning, and I do this, and I do that...I wish he would just pick up."

And I respond: "Whoa, whoa. Hold on. Why are you doing those things? So that he will finally do something? Cool. How's that feel? How's that working out for you?"

Is it working?

What I see, instead, when a woman is doing this is that she is drained and empty—running on fumes, with nothing left for herself a low sex drive, and a deep sense of misery and resentmentl. And she's still not getting what she actually wanted from the outside world. Why?

Because she's moving and attempting to source from a place of lack.

Sound familiar?

Just in case you're not yet clear, here are some little sneaky signs that you're overgiving:

- **You have gut health issues.** Parasites can be a super-deep sign that you are in unworthiness and overgiving energy. Think of parasites. What are they doing? They're taking from you. Number one sign.
- **Low sex drive.** You've got nothing left inside of you.

- **Overweight.** Why? Because you're overgiving. Your masculine energy is raising your cortisol, your stress hormone. It makes you put on belly fat.
- **You're angry.** Resentful. Stomping around. Living in a story like this: "Nobody ever shows up for me, no one ever does the things that I do for them."

Yeah, but you don't even want to be doing those things. You wouldn't be doing them in the first place if you actually knew that you are worthy. If you knew that you are loved exactly as you are; if you knew that you could just be who you're here to be, moving from a true, genuine place of love and connection (and by normal, I mean a life-giving, organic place of connection, i.e., the Self).

And this is much healthier than moving from the wounded parts of you that are trying to prove to the world (through everything that you can do and give) that someone should freaking love you. You don't need to prove that. You're inherently worthy.

So, more often than not, overgiving stems from a sense of unworthiness.

And you, beautiful woman, are worthy and whole and enough and sacred and deserving of everything that you do for everyone and more.

You don't have to prove.

You don't have to try.

You don't have to bend over backwards.

You don't have to drive around and go pick somebody up and do all these things for them just to get a breadcrumb of their love.

You don't need to do that.

Because you already are loved.

You already have everything that you need within you.

So I want you to be really honest with yourself here and ask yourself:

Where have I been overgiving?

Where have I been overextending myself?

Where have I been overfunctioning?

And understand this: Overgiving can show up as giving your man a ton of excuses for poor behaviour. That's you overfunctioning, i.e., overgiving. Bottom line: You're doing too much.

I once had a client who always drove to see her friends. They never came to her. And she was exhausted. Resentful. Over time, she realized these people weren't even really her friends. Because when she stopped giving, when she stopped doing, they didn't love her. They didn't want her.

That's not love.

And you deserve *real* love.

You deserve to be truly seen.

But you're not really seen when you're overgiving.

You literally cannot be seen when you're overgiving, because there's just too much doing going on. The doing is clouding your beingness. And who is responsible for that?

You. (Yes, really.)

So, take a look at your life:

Where do you need to pull back?

Where do you need to take all of this energy that you've been pouring into everybody else and start pouring it into yourself—your goals, your fitness, your health—the things that really matter to you?

Where in your life can you break this habit?

Now, it's going to be uncomfortable. Because you've been so accustomed to gaining love in this way. Some of you—not all. Some of you might just be in cases where you haven't been working. Okay, it probably hasn't been working. Nonetheless, when you decide to stop overgiving, you're going to be flooded with thoughts like:

"Oh no, are they going to love me?"

"Are they still going to want me?"

The answer? Yes.

The right people, the people that are meant for you, don't want you to bend over backwards and do all these things for them. They want just to love you—the essence that is you.

But that fear that you feel is valid, because you've likely been living 20, 30, 40, or 50 years in this energy.

So you really need to be graceful with yourself as you break this habit of overextending yourself (in other words, this habit of moving from a part of you that doesn't feel worthy enough).

How is this feeling? How's it all landing?

I know this chapter was dense. I'm giving you the biggest hug.

The good news is, this is literally where everything really starts to change…

Chapter 7

WHY HE WON'T COMMIT

All right. Let's get into our favourite—actually, let's be honest, our least favourite—question as women.

If you're reading this book, this question probably comes up all the time for you—maybe even endlessly.

You may wonder such things as:

Is the problem that all men are just inherently noncommittal?

Or is calling in commitment a skill or an energy?

Or some crazy secret that hasn't been passed down in my lineage?

I mean, that's what it feels like, right?

And yet, the truth is, some women consistently find themselves in these mythical things called committed relationships. Then there are other women (possibly including you, baby girl) who can't seem to get that commitment from a man whom you actually want.

I say "actually want" because you likely have the men whom you don't want chasing you down, ready to give you everything you've ever wanted and more. (And that's a phenomenon in and of itself.) So you may wonder whether or not there's something you're not yet seeing.

Well, yes: Men. You're not really seeing men.

Here's my hot take—only mine, k? I haven't heard anyone else say this and actually mean it in the way I do.

Here goes:

I truly believe men are inherently monogamous.

(I can just feel every guy in the manosphere rolling their eyes at me for this, pulling out some bogus "science" to back themselves up. Sorry, where is that "science" even from? Some podcast bro's online course?Fuck off. Am I really going to swear in this book? Well, yes, I am.)

Seriously, though, why do I believe that men are inherently monogamous?

Stay with me here. Let's just look at this logically:

Traditionally, the masculine energy protects and provides for the feminine and the child they create together in the world. If bro is out here chasing women, leaving his queen (his woman) and kin alone in their little jungle hut because he needs to be with Bethany or whoever, and then somebody comes in and attacks them or robs them, he will have taken the biggest L he could ever take.

His literal job was to protect her, take care of her, and the baby.

And this guy, by not being present…has failed hard.

Therefore, men are inherently—meaning biologically, instinctively—monogamous.

They *want* to be committed to you. They do.

For me, every time I meet a new man, I can see his inner child almost right away. And I know what he needs from the feminine.

You know what it is? Acceptance. And love.

Also, he wants to do right by her and take care of her. He wants to be "good" to her and for her.

So the next question is: If men are inherently monogamous, what makes a man commit to one woman rather than another?

It's not beauty.

It's not sex.

It's not her success.

It's not what she brings to the table.Lord, help us.

It's this one thing:

Whether she can make him feel something he has not yet felt before. The woman who can bring him into his heart—and make him feel something he has never felt—is the woman he will fall in love with and commit to.

So how do you become a woman who can make a man feel something he's never felt?

By being embodied—meaning, you need to be in your own heart, your own openness, your own truth, your own body.

If you are not in your own body, how can you bring him into his? So if you are chasing, performing, trying, doing, overfunctioning, or overgiving…you're stuck in masculine energy and not embodied in your feminine.

And he cannot feel you or see you, and thus can't fall in love with you. So, your job is to learn how to open your heart and live from the truth of your feminine being.

Luckily, that's precisely what this chapter is about. The primary reason he won't commit:

He can't see you.

He can't feel you.

And because of this, you don't bring him into his heart.

Maybe you bring him into his head. Great conversation. Logic. Amazing.

Maybe you can bring him into his dick. Great sex. Fantastic. That's fun too.

These are well and good, fun, and fabulous.

But the heart love, that's what lasts.

Do you bring him into his heart?

Do you make him feel things other than what he feels all the time, every other day? No.

Listen carefully, girlfriend: This is not a sign that you need to try harder. It's actually a sign that you need to try less and do less. Because a man who falls in love with your doing? Well…I mean, he loves your masculine energy.

Now, how do you bring a man into his heart? How do you inspire his commitment?

By living deeply within your own heart and your own body. By healing the wounded parts of you that have been so disconnected from your truth, so caught up in proving, trying, doing, performing. By finally coming back to the centred place of just embodying the truth and authenticity of all that you are.

Practically speaking? The way you inspire a man's commitment...is by being yourself.

And I know that's so cliché and sounds so silly, but it's really the truth.

Does this mean you'll inspire every man to commit to you? No. Because not every man is aligned with you.

Does that mean you will inspire *your* man to commit to you? 100%. Because he wants you, not the fake version of you. Not the version of you that you thought you needed to be for the world to love you—but the truest, most authentic version of you.

This is a version of you that you have probably lost and tucked away throughout your life. Repeatedly reaffirmed — by different people and different situations— that you could not be loved for who you are. Which is obviously not true. But it was the illusion you were living in. And it's at the root of the trauma that you've endured, which got you to where you are now, reading this book.

And the essential purpose of this book is, in fact, to bring you back to this place: The place where you are already chosen. You are already who you were created to be. You are already centred, aligned, and true to you. And inevitably, there will be so much beauty, joy, fulfillment, love, and abundance coming into your experience of life when you are living from this chosen place within you.

So the real reason why he hasn't committed? You've been too afraid to be you.

But once you are just being you, the sky's the limit.

Chapter 8

THE REAL WORK (AND WHY MOST COACHES DON'T TEACH THIS)

All right, so let's get into the real work—and why your therapy, ayahuasca ceremony, manifestation techniques, shadow work, reading personal growth books, pretending to be a Black Cat, acting unbothered, etc, etc, have not worked.

What else have you done that I haven't named? I know there's more.

Because almost every woman who comes to work with me says the same thing:

"I've done the work...but it's still not working."

And here's why:

Not everyone is well-versed in the actual rules, principles, and realities of polarity and masculine and feminine energies.

Yes, I am going to claim the title of expert here…

I see both energies so clearly, and I embody them both fully. I also heal and move through these phases of healing, both my divine feminine and my masculine energy.

The other area in which I carry a unique perspective and expertise is parts work.

I genuinely don't think that we need anything else except bodywork—ideally, including myofascial release. That is a modality of healing that I regularly receive. It's not one of my modalities as a practitioner/teacher/coach, but myofascial release, paired with the other work I do and teach my clients, is the most all-encompassing and holistic way to heal your patterns at the root.

So what exactly is the work that I do? My method involves the unconscious mind, the nervous system, and both your masculine and feminine energies.

I call this our holy trinity of healing.

What's cool about this is that we're working in three different dimensional realms:

- We're working with **the body**—the soma, aka somatics.
- We're working with **the unconscious mind**, which is what creates our external reality. We could almost view the unconscious mind as being within the first and second-dimensional realities, which then create the third dimension—3D reality. The life we live and experience day-to-day.
- And then we work within **the realm of your masculine and feminine energies,** which lie within two of the twelve laws of the universe.

And although I'm descriving these are three seperate categories, in reality they aren't seperate at all. When we do this work, all three are being healed simultaneously.

And this is whymy clients experience shifts in their reality so quickly.

I've had a client start working with me because her man had been ghosting her for three weeks, and then, after one group call in my UNION program, he texted her, telling her that he knows she's the one, he wants to marry her, and he's coming back into her life.

I've had clients whose absentee fathers message them after our call, telling them, for the first time in their lives, how proud they are.

You might not be healing or seeing the results you want in your love life,or elsewhere,because you haven't been approaching it from the right angle. Andas you'll discover in the next chapter, the right angle is healing your own emotional unavailability and your feminine energy. Both of these things are what have led you down this treacherous path of feeling you need to chase love in order to receive it.

To heal this pattern, you'll need to somatically process the stories and the trauma that are still alive in your body. Because these fragmented parts of you, the ones that feel unworthy, unloved, not enough, control 90-99% of your thoughts, actions, habits, and behaviours. And they are being projected outward into your external reality. So once we heal the part of youthat feels unworthy, you no longer need to experience a mirrored reflection of that feeling.

Because that's just no longer true for you; it's no longer a vibrational match for you.

And then we heal both your inner feminine and your masculine energies. We heal the distortions of these energies that you have been carrying, and then we allow your true inner feminine and masculine to come into union so that they can create heaven on earth together. The goal is for you to operate as a fully functioning human with both masculine and feminine energies at play.

Every single human being has both of these energies inside them. And when you come down to the truth of who you are, you are neither feminine nor masculine. You're both.

Right now in your love life, you might be asking yourself things like:

"Is sending this text feminine? Is this the feminine thing to do?"

Instead, when we do this type of work—when we tap into this holy trinity of healing—we get to a place where we finally get just to *be*. There's no more separation between inner feminine and inner masculine.

You just...*Are*.

You work when you want to work. You say what you want to say. You do what you want to do.

There is no separation, there is no confusion.

So this is usually what's missing.

It's not about being "more feminine." It's about healing the stories in your body. Healing the wounded parts of you that are alive in your unconscious mind.

Finding inner union between your masculine and feminine energies. And allowing the truest version of yourself to shine outwardly, closing the gap between who you actually are and who the world sees. Ultimately, that is a gap of emotional unavailability, and that is what we're going to dive into in the next chapter.

So, my love, it's not that you haven't been doing the work. It's possible you weren't doing the right work. And now you are, which is amazing. And that changes everything.

Chapter 9

EMOTIONAL UNAVAILABILITY: THE TRUTH ABOUT WHY YOU'RE NOT MET

This entire book is actually really about emotional availability. If you implement and allow your unconscious mind to make the shifts it wants while reading this book, you will become more emotionally available.

And I want to start by saying something that usually stops women on my socials in their tracks: "He's not the emotionally unavailable one. You are."

And here's why you probably don't see it yet. When women talk about emotional availability or unavailability, we immediately think of men. oncommittal.asual, and seeking surface-level connections. Right?

We immediately think of...Chad, right?

(I feel so bad for all the actual Chads out there, but it's always the name that comes to mind, isn't it? Ok, maybe ours is named Brad. Apologies to the good guys who have these names in real life.)

In any case, Chad or Brad is charming and fun, has a great time, takes you on dates, and is always there for the good times, the fun times, the bedroom times.

But the second that it's time to go to another level, the second that you need a tiny bit of emotional support, the second that you want more…he is no longer available. He's checked out. Gone. A ghost.

Because of this, as women, we associate emotional unavailability with men. Why? Because, unless you're a very masculine (or emotionally dissociated) woman, you're not behaving in your love life like Chad does. And this is why it's confusing.

You think you keep attracting emotionally unavailable men and you can't seem to understand how to break out of this pattern.ecause you can't yet see its true root.hich is that you yourself are emotionally unavailable.

Flash back to the chapter, "Why He Won't Commit." Remember? He can't commit to you if you can't open your heart. So emotional unavailability for a feminine woman looks nothing like what it looks like in a man. Instead, it looks like you telling your girlfriends on Saturday morning at a coffee shop that you are ready to be married, that you cannot wait to call in your man. That you are so sick and tired of attracting emotionally unavailable men…

Because what emotional unavailability truly is…is you being unavailable to the aspects of yourself that make up the true you.

Never in a million years would I have thought that I was emotionally unavailable. Me? Miss hypersensitive, Cancer rising, Mars in Scorpio? No way. Not to mention that I have always been the person who does things my way and is known for being authentic, which is a huge indicator of emotional availability.

Let me explain: If being emotionally available means you are open to the truest version of yourself, then you are the most authentic version of yourself.

Despite all that, years ago, there I was matching up consistently with emotionally unavailable men, utterly unaware of what I was doing wrong.

Over time, I came to see things more clearly. And here are some of the ways that emotional unavailability was manifesting within me:

Number one:

The things I was saying and the things I was feeling did not match up. Truthfully, I didn't even know what I was actually feeling, which is a massive sign that you are emotionally unavailable and disconnected from your truer feminine essence. How could we ever expect a man to see us and feel us if what we say and what we feel are two different things?

Number two:

I was dressing out of alignment with who I truly was.

Number three:

I was holding onto very deep pain around my heart that I was completely unaware of. I thought I had healed the trauma of my parents' deaths. I thought I had healed the deep trauma of losing the new family I'd been creating before my divorce. However, as it turned out, I hadn't truly healed from any of these things.

The fact that I grew up with a single mom, and I vowed to myself that I would never be one. Even as I write this, I feel the grief and pain in my heart, as it has been incredibly challenging for me to accept.

The loss of my family. Or the family I thought I was building. As I mentioned in the beginning, I converted religions and completely self-abandoned during the entirety of that marriage.

So the loss was less about the person and the relationship, and more about myself, my son, and the life I really wanted to have for both him and me. So I had this pain around my heart. And it's wild, because as I write this, as I finally started to process my own emotional unavailability, I can remember one of the moments in my life where I closed my heart.

I was driving home from a night shift. At that time, I was working at the hospital as a porter— asically pushing patients on gurneys to and from their appointments. It was honestly really fun. My best friend Annick and I would go job to job together, hit the gym on our break, and have the absolute best work days. I eventually went to school, became a respiratory therapist and built my career there before getting pregnant and starting my business.

But I remember driving home to whatyes was, at the time, my dream home—an old schoolhouse converted into a super cute bungalow, with so much depth and character, on 2.5 acres of land. There were horse stables and an overgrown tennis court, something I had never gotten around to revamping. I bought it with some of the inheritance I received after my mom's death, and it was way out in the country, in this place called Wakefield, outside of Ottawa. It was beautiful, right near this massive ski hill named Edelweiss.

And so I was driving home at 7 am, completely exhausted, about a year after my mom passed away. Losing somebody really close to you is a different experience entirely. Something I had no idea how to hold at 18. For those who don't yet know my story, my mom and I were very close. She was my best friend. She had me at 17, and just like in the book *Wild* by Cheryl Strayed (if you haven't read it, I love that book), she says, "I came into this world at the same age my mother left it." [7]

So goes my story, too. My mom passed away a few months before I turned 18. And the thing that's really weird about death is that initially, there's the loss…and shock. And denial and anger and all of the typical stages of grief.

But then there was the excitement of buying a house and getting a new car...this almost silver lining on the other side of this really hard thing you're going through. Things that helped me deal with the pain by staying busy, which made life…tolerable. And okay. And then there was Christmas. And little snippets of life that allowed me to survive. But then something happens.

---

[7] Cheryl Strayed, *Wild: From Lost to Found on the Pacific Crest Trail.* (New York: Alfred A. Knopf, 2012), https://www.cherylstrayed.com/wild_108676.htm.

As time goes on...you start to miss them. To miss their presence, their warmth in your life. And before that, I had never missed someone I couldn't just call or go see.

And so I was driving, and I felt this overwhelming sense—probably for the first time since she died. The first time since the first night when I found out she was gone. Because that night—that night was a night I'll never forget. And this was the first time since then thatit hit me:

I would never see her again.

And in that moment, I felt a pain I had never felt. A deep aching within the depths of my heart. A pain that can only exist when you finally face and sit with the fact that you will never see this person you so deeply loved ever again. I remember needing to pull over on the side of this long highway in the middle of the country and sob uncontrollably. I don't think I'd ever felt so much pain in my life. And I remember, in that moment, almost feeling like…

I cannot cope with this.

I cannot deal with the loss of my best friend, the woman who had been there my entire life, while my dad wasn't. The woman who told me she was proud of me for the tiniest things. The woman who was truly the most affectionate human I've ever met. The woman who honestly loved me so hard. Man, my mom loved hard. And although she was young when she had me and chaotic, and her priorities were questionable at times, she loved me. And until then, I had a deep knowing that someone would always love me and be there for me.

And at 17, I just couldn't do it. I couldn't process that. I couldn't hold that. So I shut down. I closed my heart and didn't reopen it, fully, honestly, until about 5 years ago.

Another way that you can discernthat you are emotionally unavailable is being disconnected from (and often even completely unaware of) different parts of yourself, while being completely unaware.

Let's return to those parts we talked about earlier—the ego sub-personalities that stem from trauma.

Being disconnected from those parts means you're unavailable to those parts. And when you're unavailable to those parts of you, you're ultimately unavailable to the truth of you. Unavailable to the depths of you. Unavailable to who you actually *Are*.

Here are some ways in which emotional unavailability might manifest in your life:

- Working a job you really don't like.
- Feeling unfulfilled but not yet knowing your purpose because deep down, you are emotionally unavailable to the part of you that doesn't feel good enough or worthy of the actual career that's meant for you.
- Dressing the way you think you should, instead of allowing your true feminine essence to be fully expressed in the world.

If you're working a job you don't like and that you're not meant for, we can't see you because the true you and the true career are buried deep within you. Repressed somewhere within your unconscious mind and your being…that we have yet to find. If you're meant to be wearing a thong bikini at the beach, but you're too afraid of the judgment of other people?

You are emotionally unavailable. And we can't see you. This is what I mean. Emotional unavailability is far deeper and more complex than you may have first believed.

A huge part of my process of becoming more emotionally available was allowing myself to get the tattoos that truly express who I am. You becoming emotionally available looks like you allowing yourself to be splayed open. It looks like allowing yourself to be seen. To be known. It's letting your insides shine through, and yes, it's as vulnerable as it sounds.

Over time, I've been able to reclaim large aspects of my own emotional availability. Of course, I'm not going to sit here and tell you that I'm completely emotionally available because I'm going to break down a little bit more about how and why you might not be, either. It's an ongoing healing process for all of us.

But the key to attracting emotionally available men is to become deeply available to your own heart, soul, and truth. The unprocessed pain. The different facets of your inner child. The repressed parts of yourself. . This is how we heal our unavailability.

We become aware of these things. And then we allow ourselves to take new actions based on the truth of who we really are.

We allow ourselves to dress, act, show up, and build a life that reflects the true us. Not the version of us we've been pretending to be.

Ultimately, emotional unavailability is avoidance.

Codependency is avoidance.

Anxious attachment is avoidance.

Chasing is avoidance.

When you become emotionally available to yourself, the masculine often responds by becoming available to you. When you open, he opens. When you are closed, he is closed. When you can't see yourself, he can't see you.

So the key to no longer attracting this in your life is to do the deep work to become deeply available to the truth of yourself. Because in my work, and in the energetic reality of polarity, yes, the masculine leads externally...but the feminine leads energetically. He cannot give you what you haven't yet given yourself. So if you're not available to yourself...he won't be either.

We're going to close this chapter with some journal prompts. Take some time before moving forward to start getting really clear on what you are not yet available to.

JOURNAL PROMPTS

1. In which areas of your life do you feel a general lack of fulfillment? Think career, relationships, style, where you live, etc.

____

____

____

____

____

2. Where are you still judging different aspects of yourself?

____

____

____

____

____

3. Which parts of yourself feel repressed?

____

____

____

____

____

4. What pain/heartbreak from your past do you have yet to process? How can you start to let it go?

5. How have you been showing up in ways that feel out of alignment with who you truly are?

6. What feels too scary to express or admit?

Chapter 10

THE MYTH OF SOFTNESS

Being feminine doesn't inherently mean soft. In some ways, yes.

In the way of being emotionally available.

Being seen.

Being supple.

Being penetrable.

But not necessarily in the sense of being soft-spoken, unopinionated, etc.

I mean, sure. You can be feminine and soft-spoken. But you can also be feminine and fight against injustices in our world. You can also be feminine and decide that you've had enough of how someone has treated you, and choose to finally take a stand for yourself.

The reason softness is associated with femininity is that it's non-threatening.

Because it allows people—men—to act in ways that are not right…and women have no other choice than to deal with it.

To me, it feels like an agenda to keep women out of their power, out of their truth, in the same way that other agendas keep men out of their personal, masculine power and their truth. Men also feel unable to stand up for themselves, their women, their children, and the world.

We live in a world full of passivity, pushed on us by society, for purposes I believe are about control.

Yes, we're going down a bit of a rabbit hole here. Still, I truly do believe there are forces and agendas at play to keep both men and women out of their masculine and feminine forms...and truest forms of power, which involves us finding union together.

This is why we see gender wars.

This is why we see attacks on women's rights. Attacks on masculinity.

And then all of this stuff hating on masculinity.

It's a war.

It was curated.

And it's up to us to break out of it.

So yes. You being "soft" and feeling like you are not allowed to speak up for what's not right is inevitably going to enable people—men, the world, other women—to walk all over you.

Is the feminine meant to be felt and seen and trusting and loving and nurturing?

Yes.

Yes. She is.

And you, being in wounds and feeling like you need to protect yourself, harbouring deep anger, bitterness, and resentment towards the masculine and allowing it to come out in all sorts of ways, is not soft, nor is it healed or whole...or holy.

It's wounded.

And so, if we are to talk about softness in the sense of you being armoured and bitter and angry and letting all of your anger towards your father out on a random man on a random afternoon who's holding the door open for you, that is not only not soft…

That is not right.

Nor is that helpful for any of what's at play in the world.

But if we are to talk about softness as in you tolerating disrespect…

Or allowing abuse…

Or seeing something happen in your community or country and just standing by, knowing full well in your heart that it is not right…

That is not feminine, nor the type of softness I am recommending.

That is disempowerment.

And this is why you cannot allow these teachings around the feminine being soft to take you out of your truth.

Every single human being is given discernment and is given things in their hearts that they are meant to stand for, fight for, and ultimately live for.

So this entire narrative around the feminine is likely—potentially—keeping you in unhealthy situations and dynamics in the name of false femininity.

There is a way to be in your truth and power without being wounded. There is actually a massive difference between moving from truth and power versus from pain.

A woman stepping in to protect a child is a rightful act.

And it is not a sign that she is not soft or feminine.

If anything, it is a sign of her femininity.

A woman yelling at her man in the middle of the streets, lacking grace and any form of control over her emotions—moving from a wounded part of her—is not feminine.

Once again, it is wounded.

We really need to dissect and understand that there are always deeper layers to all of the actions at play.

Again, that same woman who is stepping in to protect a child could look the same as a woman yelling at you in the grocery store. However, the intention and the source of this action are entirely different.

One could be a feminine truth.

The other, a wound.

So don't let this myth of softness deter you from aligning with who you are as a woman.

I have a client who fights for animal freedom and animal injustice, and she is deeply, deeply feminine. And in those moments, believe me, she is not soft in any conventional sense of the word.

But man, oh man, would she be perceived as a goddess. A warrior in the flesh. Here to bring truth, love, and justice to the world. And personally, I don't know that there is anything more feminine than that.

And I think on a deep psychological level, we all understand that.

I'm literally remembering Xena the Warrior Princess.

I'm thinking of Lara Croft.

It's like…we all know that the true feminine is multifaceted.

Whole.

All-encompassing of all life itself.

And in some ways, Lara Croft and Xena the Warrior Princess are, in fact, soft externally because they are hard and strong internally.

They are soft, supple, and feminine externally.

Strong and ruthless internally.

This is a strong woman.

This is a soft woman.

The hard woman externally is a woman who is incredibly wounded, insecure…

And, at least for the moment, internally weak.

The person who is consistently offended…

Who needs to defend their position all the time…

Who you feel like you have to walk on eggshells around…

That is somebody who is prickly externally because internally there is no fortress.

Internally, there is no strength.

So we want you to embody the true softness you are meant to embody, the softness of being in your body and allowing yourself to express yourself. We want you to let your insides shine outside, which is an extremely vulnerable position.

Again, think of a woman who's fighting for something that she truly believes in.

That is a very vulnerable experience.

The experience of sharing an opinion is much like writing a book or sharing your art.

You are allowing something internal to be seen, felt, and experienced externally.

That is a woman who is penetrable, because we are penetrating through the façade to see the truth of her.

Through her ideas.

Through her writing.

Through her fashion.

Through her art.

Through whatever it is.

That is a soft woman.

That is the softness that we're looking for.

Not hiding your heart.

Not hiding your true expression.

Not hiding what it is that you believe about this world under the guise of being more feminine, not wanting to appear too intelligent, not wanting to intimidate a man, or whatever else you've been taught...

This is the opposite of the true feminine.

Because it is the opposite of seen, meaning you've created this hard shell externally because internally you can't cope with the rejection or whatever might come from being so deeply seen and felt.

So the true definition of softness is:

To allow your insides to shine outside—whatever that might look like—as long as what we are shining from the inside on the outside is truth...and is healed and whole.

And that woman that I talk about, who's very prickly?

She is ultimately showing her insides on the outside...but what she is showing us is pain.

Trauma.

Heartbreak.

Mistrust.

Anger.

Bitterness.

Resentment.

And that is seen and felt.

So when you see these videos and when you hear this stuff about femininity and softness, this is what it's about.

It's not that you need to placate yourself.

It's not that you need to keep your mouth shut at all times.

It's not that you have to be soft-spoken and that you are never allowed to stand for anything or raise your voice or anything of the sort.

No.

It's that you are meant to purify that which has been tainted and traumatized and wounded by your experiences of the past, by society, by that which isn't the true you.

So how can you allow the world to start to feel the real you?

How can you allow yourself to go through the process of softening on the outside—of being happy, of smiling, of being joyful, of being honest about what you believe, about being honest about what you're feeling…

While knowing that internally, you are going to be ok.

Because that's what it's really about.

The most feminine woman is internally the strongest woman.

So, where can you find more internal strength, so you can soften in real feminine ways?

Chapter II

EMBODIMENT > STRATEGY

I'm honestly exhausted by the topic of feminine energy. All of a sudden, everyone's an expert, and yet very few actually reach the depths of what it truly is.

Many people teaching about feminine energy look to the past, before the feminist agenda, thinking that how women behaved then reflected true feminine energy. Women, at home, being mothers, homemakers, baking and cooking, submissive to their husbands who worked in a growing industrial revolution, angry and cut off from their own heart, spirit, creativity, and feminine energy, as though that is where we are meant to go back to.

Why do we look at a time when husbands beat their wives, fathers couldn't tell their sons they loved them, had affairs with their secretaries, and institutionalized their wives if they had an orgasm, as a proper reflection of feminine energy?

How is that our ideal example?

Is being a mother and homemaker feminine? Sure, yes. It can be.

However, energetically, being a mother to children under five years old is actually mostly an extremely masculine experience. You are in constant action and doing. This is why the higher archetypes of the feminine, as in the Mother/Queen, are archetypes of union. In other words, integration of both masculine and feminine energies.

Cooking and cleaning are not, in fact, feminine.

They're masculine activities because they involve action, exertion, and organization/planning.

Feminine energy is deeper than just domesticity. If we want to know the feminine truly, then we should look back much further, to when women roamed the earth barefoot, naked, free bleeding, child in hand.

Women connected to their truth, womb, blood, guts, and bones. Women who could call up arms as easily as they could nurture their infant. Women who brought wisdom and codes to their warrior men. Women who didn't shrink at the power of his voice and presence. Women who could stand by his side.

The point is, feminine energy isn't a game, a prop, a costume, or a performance.

It isn't an apron you can put on.

A pie you can bake.

Listen, I make a mean pie. And I can cook. At Christmas time, we are all shocked at the spread I lay out. But that isn't what makes me feminine.

And it isn't what makes you feminine, either.

Becoming more "feminine" in the real sense of the word will likely be the deepest spiritual initiation you ever embark on. Truly.

So what does feminine embodiment[8] actually feel like?

It feels like knowing exactly what to say when he texts you, because there is no other option but for you to just be you. It feels like finally being able to make a home inside

---

[8] Joan Christler and Ingrid Johnston-Robledo, *Woman's Embodied Self: Feminist Perspectives on Identity and Image, 1st ed.* (Washington, DC: American Psychological Association, 2018), https://psycnet.apa.org/record/2017-32522-000.

your body. It feels like experiencing deep intimacy with him without ever wondering how your belly or body looks, as you are so engulfed in the pleasure and experience itself. It feels like knowing you are okay, with or without him, but choosing to love him with your heart wide open.

It feels like your head back, arm stretched out the window, wind in your hair, laughing, listening to your favourite song, driving up the coast, smelling the salt in the air.

It feels like freedom. In all its forms. Freedom from the exhaustion, the trying, the doing, the proving. And finally, finding solace and peace in this tiny moment we call our lives.

And this is why all the $5 "Get the guy" PDFs and how-to-be-more-feminine tips and tricks aren't working.

Because there is no one way to be feminine.

There is only your way. And your way involves coming to terms with who you actually are. It involves letting go of all that's been keeping you in masculine energy and/or inauthenticity.

So, given all that, let's look at some of the things that are keeping you from being embodied in your natural feminine energy:

- The need to protect yourself
- Your defence mechanisms
- Needing to prove that you're right
- Needing to prove the world wrong
- Your fears of judgment
- Your fears of rejection
- Your fears of being alone
- Your fears of what they'll think of you
- The part of you that doesn't feel good enough
- The part that doesn't feel worthy

- Never having been loved for who you are
- The part that doesn't feel wanted
- Your fears of being seen

Ultimately, all of these things keep you prickly, armoured, defensive, and in need of protection. All of these things make you really soft, oftentimes insecure, on the inside, and hard—armoured and shelled—on the outside.

The path to becoming truly feminine is to build internal strength, be resilient, know yourself deeply, and not be affected by what others say or think about you.

To know that you have your own back.

To know that you are going to protect yourself, cherish yourself, and treat yourself like you are the most precious creature in the entire world. (Because you are.)

And thus, you will only place yourself in situations that mirror the deep love you have for yourself, allowing you to find softness externally.

It is a strong inner masculine that allows you to embody a soft feminine energy.

This is why, oftentimes, these tips and tricks that you find online aren't helping because they aren't allowing you to cultivate the necessary safety and security you need to soften.

And there is no way that I am going to allow you to sit in a place of disempowerment and believe that the only way to become feminine is to first have an external masculine force in your life.

To stay in this state is to remain in a lower archetype of feminine—the princess archetype—or rather, the maiden…or the wounded maiden, I should say. A woman who needs something outside of herself first, to become that which she was created to be.

The Wounded Maiden.

A woman caught in victimization and the need for someone to save her. This is the lower version of you, made up of those lower parts of you.

She's the woman who walks into a room and demands everyone's attention. The woman who needs constant reassurance. Who wants mommy, daddy, or a man to come in and save her. This woman is constantly blaming others or external circumstances for why she hasn't yet created the life she truly wants.

The wounded maiden is a woman without a strong internal mother. Unable to roll up her sleeves and step into the higher archetypes of the feminine.

She is flailing around, unable to control herself or her emotions.

This is the woman in your life who always has something wrong. She can never seem to pay her bills or rent on time.

(I'm not judging, we've all been this woman. We know this woman. We love this sweet baby girl. I, too, had to heal my own wounded feminine energy and become the mother I needed to become the woman I am today. And that healing? It's an ever-flowing process that is continuing.)

The mature feminine, the queen understands that true feminine power is within and that to wait for a man to appear for her to soften is to stay a victim to her external reality…and to stay in a state of girlhood.

The true process of becoming feminine first involves reclaiming your inner king and your inner father.

When you integrate your inner feminine and inner masculine, your inner queen/mother and inner king/father, you won't need games, the realm of dating and relationships. Because not only will they not last, but they will never create the deep, all-encompassing love that you so deeply crave.

Games feed off of other people's egoic, wounded parts. If you create a relationship from games, you are creating a relationship from ego. And there is no love in ego. Any man that you attract by being unbothered, or a black cat, or saying the "perfect thing," is a man who will never love the depths of you.

And despite what you might see on social media from other teachers or coaches...

Men do love deeply. Surprise, surprise—they are human beings capable of love. My son literally gives me hundreds of kisses daily. He is the most cuddly little boy I have ever met. He is so sweet, so kind, so sensitive, so loving—and also so logical, so brave, such a leader, so intelligent. He has all of the qualities of a (currently) tiny little king.

This doesn't go away as they get older. Not naturally, anyway. It goes away as our society conditions men to hate their emotions and hate all things feminine. Many little boys quickly learn:

Don't cry.

Don't be a pussy.

Don't be all the things that women are.

It's no wonder we have a society of men who are afraid to admit that, at times, they cry, that they are romantic, and that they love deeply and completely. And so what the man that you are meant to call in needs is your depth, your heart, and your soul. And that will never be seen, felt, or experienced within strategies and the games you've been taught to play.

Feminine energy isn't an act.

It's your truest state of being.

You don't need to do anything to become her.

You actually need to stop doing.

You need to put your sword down.

You need to heal your trust wounds.

You need to heal your past heartbreaks.

You need to heal the beliefs you have about men and the world.

You need to allow yourself, your creativity, and your voice to be seen and heard.

You need to know yourself and accept yourself exactly as you are.

You need to walk through the world without fear:

Embodied in your values, in your insights, in your truth, in your knowledge, in your heart, in your sensuality, in your beauty, in your bigness, in your enough-ness, and in all that you were created to be.

You need to stand proud and unwavering in the eyes and judgment of others.

You need to have your own back.

You need to be the light in your own life.

This is how you embody your feminine energy. By finally deciding that who you are at the core has always been worth loving, exactly as you are.

JOURNAL PROMPTS

1. Where in your life are you hard or guarded externally? What are you trying to protect?

___

___

___

___

___

___

2. Where do you need to step up in your own life and relationships to protect yourself and build a stronger inner fortress?

3. How can you begin to trust that you have your own back, so you can begin to let down your walls?

4. Where have you confused softness with weakness?

5. How can you learn to let go of people's perception of you and start to take things less personally?

6. What do you genuinely believe in or stand for that you've been afraid to express?

7. Where can you allow more of your true self to be seen?

Chapter 12

DETACHMENT VS. AVOIDANCE

The world of social media is obsessed with detachment. Actually, the worlds of social media and manifestation are both obsessed with detachment. I get it, the law of detachment is universal. And it is truly important. And yet, we need to make sure that we are not falling into patterns of avoidance or spiritually bypassing to be in our feminine energy.

The law of detachment is really the law of detaching from outcomes. Because the more that you want something, the more you are activating the energy of not having it, and therefore messing with its manifestation in your reality. The energy of detachment, on the other hand, makes space for things to show up and manifest for you.

Honestly, based on the messages I regularly receive from women, most of you are already total experts in the realms of manifestation and detachment. Many of you are already practicing manifestation and detachment to either call in your specific person or to try to heal the relationship patterns you've had.

And yes, we do want to detach from a specific outcome and a specific person.

And this can be really challenging, depending on your attachment style[9] and the general attachments and meanings you make about this person choosing or not choosing you. This really is the angle that I want to go off on, because this is the angle that allows you to actually detach, not pretending to detach while just moving into deeper avoidance with yourself, which inevitably and almost always creates external avoidance from the man or the people around you.

If we look back at our mirrored reality, you will see that if you are avoiding yourself, i.e., if you're running from yourself, he will be running from you.

Let's go over what attachment isn't:

- Pretending not to care.
- Acting like you don't want a relationship with this person.
- Spiritually bypassing (aka ignoring the deeper feelings that are happening when you don't hear from them or when things don't work the way that you want) in the name of staying detached.
- Acting unbothered when realistically you are very bothered.

All of this falls under the umbrella of avoidance.

Because all of these things are you avoiding your own feminine heart and your own feminine truth, which means that you will be unseen and unfelt by the man, by yourself, and the world at large.

In the name of love and relationships and commitment, I actually think you are far better off admitting that you feel anxious, or admitting that you really care, or are scared to lose him, than pretending that you aren't feeling any of those things.

Because pretending is a form of masculine energy, it's doing, and it's stemming from ego and a façade, which will end up pushing the man you are so fervently trying to "manifest" further away from you, because there is no genuine intimacy.

---

[9] Kendra Cherry, "4 Attachment Styles in Relationships," Verywell Mind, November 17, 2025, https://www.verywellmind.com/attachment-styles-2795344.

Intimacy = in-to-me-see?

And without you being connected to your own heart, he can't fall in love with you.

So the reason the detachment you've been practicing hasn't been working is likely because you've been in avoidance, versus being genuinely detached from the outcome.

So how do we get to that place of genuine detachment? This is the magic question.

Unless you're an actress, I doubt you want to continue performing for the rest of your life and pretending that you aren't feeling the way that you're feeling in an attempt to get love. That honestly just sounds exhausting.

So let's go over what true feminine detachment is.

If you are practicing performative detachment, you are losing yourself. You are avoiding yourself. You are moving further and further from your truth, your alignment, and the woman you are meant to be.

And as you move further and further from your deepest Self, your person ultimately moves further and further from you.

What we want is for you to be in union and complete alignment with yourself, your true self, and still be detached from an outcome. That's the true feminine path.

You can be outcome-driven in business.

You can be outcome-driven in your goals.

You can be outcome-driven in your fitness, racing, and whatever you want.

But not in your relationship.

You need to learn how to switch between your masculine and feminine energies and when to bring each into play.

Your goals, your business, and your career all need your masculine energy. Great.

Your relationship needs your feminine energy, unless you want to be with a more flowy, artistic, creative, "feminine" man, maybe one who surfs and is really chill and is going to cook for you and play guitar and serenade you. At the same time, you make all the money (which is completely OK in every way!) Unless you want that type of man, you need to learn to leave your masculine energy and your outcomes at the door.

You wouldn't feel the need to pretend to be unbothered or to act detached and act like you don't care about the outcome...if you weren't trying to get a certain result.

Do you see what I'm saying?

You're far better off just being honest about the fact that you're trying to get outcomes, trying to get him to chase you, and all of these things than putting on this whole façade that you're detached...when really, you're still playing the same old games of looking for safety through patterns of control.

You can't control how he is showing up. You can't control the fact that he's not committing to you, not calling you, not doing this, not doing that...

You're unable to control the external reality and feel safe in how he's showing up because you don't yet know how to surrender to your feminine and live a life detached from outcomes. You then take all the control you could have been putting towards him and start controlling your own actions in an attempt to control how he shows up.

Somebody tell me how that is feminine and surrendered.

It's an illusion of femininity.

On the outside, you probably do look feminine. You're telling your girlfriends, "Oh, I'm totally detached, it doesn't matter whether he calls or not, I'm totally fine..."

But deep down, you're playing this game of thinking that if you say nothing and don't post anything on your stories and take all your energy away from him, he is going to want to call and message you—not realizing that you're in complete avoidance of what's actually going on in your body, spiritually bypassing and missing the entire point.

What we want is for you to genuinely not care whether or not he calls or wants you.

Why?

Because you are not meant to be living at the mercy of the external reality, let alone a mere mortal man.

This is not freedom.

This is not life.

This is not your purpose.

And to continue to live this way is to keep siphoning from your own Eros, your own life force energy, your own turn-on, in an attempt to get something that was never meant to fill you.

So let's fix this inversion that you, my beautiful girl, have found yourself in...and flip you right side up.

The first step is to clarify why you are attached to him choosing you, committing to you, or wanting you, however you want to see that. Let's get clear on why you're attached to the outcome you want and why you need that to happen on a deep, unconscious level.

This is where you need to reach a new level of intimacy and relationship with yourself. You must be really honest with yourself right now, even if it's uncomfortable.

What do you think his choosing you will do for you?

What do you think will happen in your life once he chooses/claims you?

What would it make you feel if he didn't choose you?

Okay. These three questions are going to be the first step out of the prison you have found yourself in.

And I know, because I found myself in these places. And holy moly is it ever exhausting to be living your entire life basically orbiting around whether or not some dude chooses you.

And no disrespect to the beautiful man that you're going to fall in love with and create an incredible life with…but he's still just a man.

And you're giving far too much power to what is not even everlasting.

We're not meant to find our power and worth in another human. Otherwise, we will never truly be free.

So the way to become truly detached is to no longer need or make meaning out of what somebody else is doing or not doing. We have to take away the power that we gave them.

You have to make a choice.

Learn to trust life and God, Source, whatever you want to call it, and not only believe, but truly embody, that what is meant for you will find you.

The path of the true feminine is to be so focused on your own life, your own turn-on, your own goals, your own fulfillment, your own timeline…that you ultimately live your life almost as though you have this open door that a man can either come into or not.

And if he is the right man, you will love him, and you will devote yourself to him in so many beautiful ways, and you will experience so many different facets of yourself through this relationship.

But regardless of him, you are still worthy.

You are still enough.

You are still whole.

You can still stand on your own two feet.

You still have goals, dreams, ambitions. Things that matter deeply to you.

Because no man should be able to change that or take that away from you.

And if you're allowing him to, then, again, that's why you're reading this book. And this is what we are shifting and changing.

Furthermore, the true path of a man choosing you and committing to you for life is for you to be so deeply committed to yourself and your own life that he ultimately has no choice but to mirror that back to you.

And if we come back to the law of detachment, the masculine's number one value is freedom. He needs to feel free.

When you avoid going into patterns of control (because, again, even if you're acting unbothered, he can feel the subtle layers of your attempts to control the entire experience), this takes away the space for him to embody his masculine energy with you. It removes the opportunity for him to step up, be there for you, and be the man you need him to be. Why? Because your energy is taking up all of the space in the relationship, since you're not yet in your feminine energy.

So this freedom, and you no longer needing him to choose you or claim you for you to feel whatever came up in those three questions, is the literal freedom that he needs to choose you for a lifetime.

Remember, if you are attached to a specific outcome with this man, what you are implying is that without him, you don't have whatever it is you think that outcome will give you, and that means you are in an energy of lack.

The law of attraction states that you attract that which you are.

And on other deeper levels, as we discussed earlier, your entire embodiment is pushed out into the world.

So if you need him and are attached to him choosing you so that you feel good, worthy, enough, whatever it is, you are ultimately implying that you don't feel good, worthy, enough, etc., as it is.

And nothing in this external world can give us what we have not yet embodied internally.

So learning to detach is the path of the feminine.

Because it's a path of finally finding wholeness while also finding refuge and trust in life itself.

Detaching means you finally let go.

Finally surrender.

Finally, believe that you are a precious being, worthy of all of the beautiful things that life has to offer, and that there is nothing you need to do to receive these things.

And spoiler alert: You can't fake your way into detachment or feminine energy.

You have to heal your way there.

It's the only way.

Chapter 13

SURRENDERING TO THE LOVE THAT'S MEANT FOR YOU

I believe that one of the main reasons women and men are not in a union or relationship they could be is that they are caught up in patterns of control and ideas about what they want in love, as though they actually know what's best for them.

This is probably confusing. You may be thinking, "Kelsey, this whole time you've been helping us get clear on who we are and what we want…and now you're here saying that we don't know what we want in love?"

Yes, that is precisely what I'm saying.

And I can see how that sounds confusing.

But I'm sharing this truth with you, anyway, because I've personally had to learn this lesson so many times, in so many different ways.

Learning and relearning this lesson stems from an inability to trust life and God, and that, in some way, somehow, you will be taken care of better than you could've ever possibly taken care of yourself.

But I know it's tough to believe this when we have spent so much of our lives finding proof of all of the ways that we were not taken care of. The ways we were not met or did not get what we wanted.

I, for example, spent most of my life hoping and wishing and praying that my dad would come back into my life and be a father to me.

When I was about three or four, he left my life. My mom was 17 when she met my dad, who was 18. He had recently been released from jail for armed robbery (with a pocket knife, I might add, which is pretty epic if you ask me and almost sweet, especially if you knew my dad). He wasn't a bad guy, really. He had an issue with drugs, and by issue, I mean he spent his entire life struggling with addiction to crack, heroin, and cocaine.

His father was an alcoholic, and he grew up in a really abusive household. From what I understand, he was riddled with intense feelings of embarrassment about who he was and the issues he dealt with.

I spent my entire life praying that he would come back.

My mom had a lot of boyfriends. A lot.

I would get so attached to each one. I loved some of them so much, and yet all I really wanted was my father. I just wanted to know that he could get clean, make an effort, and come back into my life and be the dad I always needed him to be.

When I was 16 or so, my mom and stepdad took me out for a run (this was how we bonded. It was pretty cute), and on our run, they shared with me that they had found out that my dad had contracted HIV. I wasn't sure how to process that information.

Fast-forward six to twelve months later, my nanny (my grandmother) and my cousin both came to visit my mom and me while we were living with my stepdad and stepsister.

The occurrences that happened before my mom's death were honestly bizarre, and in hindsight, such a clear indication that something huge was about to happen in my life. Not only did my dad's family come in contact with me again, but my mom's estranged sister showed up on her doorstep too, about a week before she died.

It's like…as much as life can be a mystery, it also almost plays out like a perfect movie with a perfect plot, giving us clues and signs of what must be to come.

I digress, though.

I want to go back to my dad: That's the point of this chapter.

My mother passed away about a year after that conversation, and a few years after her death, I got in contact with my dad and met with him in Toronto for coffee.

I was 22 years old. I remember putting on this cute sundress, shoes, and this adorable leather jacket I bought from Garage, and feeling so scared, excited, and nervous to finally be building a relationship with this person I had wanted my entire life.

I had seen photos of him, but I had no idea how tall he was or anything. So I stood in the Starbucks at Yonge and Dundas with no idea who I was actually looking for.

As I stood there, this man, who seemed about my height (I was wearing high heels), said hi. I didn't really know what to do next (as I don't generally engage with 40-year-old men), so I just kind of said hi back and then walked away. Only to hear him say, "Kelsey." It was him.

We had coffee, sat across from each other, and I remember him directly asking me if I hated him.

I started to cry.

That was never a feeling I had felt towards my dad growing up.

I did feel anger later, after he died. It was only then I realized that within this deep wound of abandonment and fear of not being chosen, I didn't let myself be angry or disappointed or dissatisfied with the masculine out of fear that it would prevent him from choosing me.

But at that time, in that café on a Saturday afternoon in July with my dad…No, I had never felt angry towards him.

I responded, "No, I don't hate you. I'm not mad at you. You and my mom were kids. I've never felt anything bad towards you."

I ended up walking him to his AA meeting.

We spoke two other times on the phone (collect calls from him).

I had his mom's number in my purse for about 6 months, and for some reason, I just couldn't bring myself to call, even though I felt his energy so close to me the entire time. One morning, I woke up after a night out with my girlfriends and had an overwhelming sense that it was time.

When I called, I heard my Nana's voice on the phone.

I asked her if my dad was there, and she said, "Kelsey, your dad died six months ago."

I felt like the wind had been knocked out of me.

I felt the deepest sense of shame and regret knowing that I had an opportunity to reach out to him, and I didn't. Knowing that maybe we could've built a relationship…but we didn't.

The people closest to me knew that, although my mom had passed away 10 years prior, I had never really truly processed it. In all honesty, I really only started processing it in the last 3–4 years because that was all the capacity I had.

The advice I was given was to feel this fully and completely.

And I did.

For three days, I lay in some of my closest friends' arms. Held by my sisters.

Then wept.

And felt.

A different sense of loss.

Different in the sense that yes, I lost both my mom and my dad. But losing somebody that you never had a chance to love…that's a different kind of feeling.

During the months after that experience, I started to really process the repressed anger that I had towards this man who was never able to show up and step up for me.

This experience, as all of our experiences shape us, ended up hardwiring me into feeling as though I was never enough for love. For a dad.

It had me feel like I was less than all the other girls who had their dads in their lives.

About a year later, I was having a girls' night. It was the middle of the night, and I was down in the kitchen pouring myself a glass of water when, almost like a lightning bolt, it hit me:

I was never, ever going to wait for a man to choose me.

At that moment, I dropped the glass, and it shattered all over the kitchen floor.

One of my girlfriends came down.

She stood across from me with all of the shattered glass between us and asked me if I was okay.

And I just remember, shaking, telling her:

I spent my entire life wanting and waiting for my dad to show up, only to find out that he died before ever trying to build a relationship with me. And that I would rather die than wait for another man to choose me.

I don't want to offend anyone with that last statement.

At this time in my life, I have no anger, disdain, or any ill feelings towards my dad in any way, shape, or form. Nor do I still victimize myself by the choices he made, as I am fully aware that how he showed up (or rather didn't show up) as a father had absolutely nothing to do with me and everything to do with him, who he was, and, more importantly, how he felt about himself.

People don't treat you how they feel about you. They treat you how they feel about themselves.

But the moral of the story, and something that has taken me a really long time to understand, is that we don't actually know what is best for us.

As a little girl, my dad was all I wanted, and yet, for some reason, I genuinely do believe that God made it so that he was not in my life. I can only imagine what growing up with an addicted parent would have been like. I have so much love, compassion, and empathy for addiction, truly, yet for some reason, on my path and on my journey, what I wanted was not what was best for me.

And what I needed to surrender to…was what life was actually giving me.

Likewise, so much of what you think you might want in love and in a relationship might not actually be what you need.

We're not meant to control every aspect of our lives.

We're not meant to choose it all.

This is why I believe that making lists of your "perfect partner" and all of these qualities and characteristics is actually not serving you in any way, shape, or form. The focus should be on how you want to feel.

How can you surrender and trust that Life, God, the Universe, Source (whatever you want to call it) is taking care of you?

And knows you better than you know yourself.

And knows the perfect person for you, the perfect person that is far from perfect, but who will show you and teach you:

How to love.

How to forgive.

How to show up for another human being.

How to have compassion.

How to have empathy.

How to have boundaries and standards.

How to use your voice.

How to support.

And how to love in the ways that we were always created to love.

So, can you let go of your list?

Can you let go of what you think you want and actually open yourself up to what you're being given?

The type of man you're being given. The kind of man that might actually be right for you. Good for you. Great for you, even.

Chapter 14

THE MOST IMPORTANT PIECE

We cannot talk about feminine embodiment and breaking your patterns of chasing without touching on the most important aspect of how you could ever possibly surrender, let go, and trust that you will find love without needing to prove, shift, perform, chase, contort, and whatever else you've been accustomed to.

And that is your trust in life—in God—in the unseen.

I want to start by saying that I've never been particularly religious. I mean, yes, we went over my 3 years as a convert before the birth of my son, but beyond that, I was never religious. I wasn't raised religious. I wasn't baptized as a child.

My mom did yoga and meditated, and we were "spiritual." She raised me with a Japanese philosophy called *Kaizen*, focused on becoming better every single day. Something that has shaped me in the most beautiful ways, as I have a constant yearning for improvement and self-actualization. And something that I have needed to break free from, as I have consistently felt throughout my life that nothing was ever enough.

Between *Kaizen* and my mom's continuous, "How could you have gone from an A+ to an A-?" to "Find a better word," when I would eventually say something as a teenager, I developed a deep belief that if I could just do more or be more, then things would end up the way I wanted or the way I had hoped.

Now, although we weren't religious, we did use the word "God," and throughout this chapter, I will use that word. In my world and my belief system, God could be seen as the thing within all things. You can use the word "Universe," "Source," or whatever feels best to you.

You can also choose to reclaim the word God without needing to be of any religion, just as you can be of any religion and still read this book and resonate with it. I think our relationship with our Creator, just as with all things, is deeply personal and unique to each of us, and a necessary part of your process for embodying your truest feminine essence.

So how does one begin to trust Life?

Do you decide that things only feel good when they're going the way you want?

Or can you sink into every moment, every up and down in your life, and find gratitude for where you are and where it's potentially taking you? I think the vast majority of human suffering, and the vast majority of why women lose their feminine essence, is because they've learned that life isn't safe. That it is only meant to feel good. That they can only be happy and find joy when everything is going exactly as planned, something that rarely ever occurs.

So often, women come to me, unhappy because their man isn't loving them properly when in actuality, he is loving her, deeply, but because she doesn't feel safe within herself and within life, her need for control has her rejecting the oil changes he does for her out of love as it doesn't match the exact picture of what she had imagined he was supposed to love her by. Something that not only prevents her from being her feminine self, at peace, and enjoying the life she's meant to enjoy, but erodes the relational intimacy between her and her man, as he feels like what he does is never enough.

The thing with life, and that we need to understand about life, is that it isn't perfect, nor is it controllable, nor is it going to feel good all the time. And it's okay. Being alive means feeling the fullness that all of life has to offer.

I remember standing in the shower, with the water running down my face, the night after we all found out that there was no brain activity left in my mom and that she'd need to be unplugged, with the most gaping hole I'd ever felt in my heart. As I stood there, numb to the shock of what was happening, while feeling completely heart-cracked open down my entire chest, I felt, amidst the deepest pain, the presence of God over and in my life in ways I almost cannot describe. It's as though, in my darkest hour, I felt held and loved and remembered I had always been held, cherished, and loved by my Creator.

Life is there.

There is no good or bad.

There only *is*.

To let go is to know it isn't meant to look a certain way. There are no shoulds. The only way through this life is to feel as though you are free-falling out of a plane—and in that surrender, you are finally free.

It's our control that makes life hard.

Our plans.

Our regrets, what-ifs, constant overthinking, and resistance to what is that make us suffer.

Not life itself.

Life itself is just that.

Life.

Within creation, there is destruction and chaos, and there is absolutely nothing you could ever possibly do to change that.

It's bigger than you.

Vaster than you.

More intelligent than you.

To be feminine is to lean back, trust, nestle ourselves into the arms of God and *know*, deep within our bones, that something *does* want the best for us.

But that doesn't mean it's going to look the way you want it to. And yes, that's hard because you likely have deep wounds of disappointment from when you were a little girl, and it's hard to understand that *not* having what you want is somehow "right" or the way it's supposed to be.

And yet that is what it is to embark on the spiritual practice of being feminine, a path I would, although I obviously haven't done this, would honestly compare to any other spiritual practice.

Trust.

Trust that it's right.

Respect God, respect the masculine, respect life and what it is giving you.

Trust that it's what's needed.

Reframe moments of "waiting" as opportunities to build patience.

Reframe aspects of putting in work towards your goals without any reward as character-building.

See the positive in all things.

Look at the bigger picture.

Borrow from biblical principles that, although bad things might happen, God will use all situations for good. Something spoken about thoroughly and powerfully in the movie *The Shack* (2017), directed by Stuart Hazeldine.[10]

Look back on your life.

Be honest: Although you may have gone through extreme hardship, you are here, with me, in these pages, reading this book. Which means, on some level, you are okay. Maybe not emotionally, maybe not spiritually, and maybe not physically, and for that I am sorry. I am here extending so much love and empathy to you, but you are still, in ways, okay.

And to remember that is to remember that something bigger than you must be taking care of you.

It's really hard for clients to come to me and leave a container with me without having rebuilt a relationship with God, the Universe, or their Creator.

A large portion of women who work with me heal their religious trauma and reclaim their use of the word God, and restore their position as daughters. A position that allows you to rest and surrender, knowing that as a daughter, your father will inevitably and always want the absolute best for you.

Notice I didn't say to give you everything you want when you want because that isn't always what's best. An entire pint of Häagen-Dazs at 9 pm on a Sunday probably isn't the best thing for you. Giving you that new job you interviewed for, prepared for, showed gratitude for, and feel ready for, probably is.

I firmly believe that you cannot embody your true feminine nature without this. Without this, you will continue to perpetuate the wounds you've been trying so hard to heal:

- That you are alone

---

10 *The Shack,* directed by Stuart Hazeldine (Lionsgate Films, 2017), https://www.youtube.com/watch?v=CL0yUbSS5Eg.

- That you need to do everything yourself
- That you need to push and force to get what it is that you want
- That you aren't taken care of
- That you aren't worthy
- That you cannot just be

The wounds that sit at the root of why you have been chasing love and connection outside of you, that prevent you from finally embodying an identity of being chosen, and that, once healed, are your ultimate freedom from that which has been plaguing you month after month.

Faith is the key to your feminine embodiment.

"For truly I tell you, if you have faith the size of a mustard seed, you will tell this mountain, 'Move from here to there,' and it will move. Nothing will be impossible for you." (Matthew 17:20 [NIV])

PART III:
THE CHOSEN FREQUENCY

Chapter 15

BECOMING THE CHOSEN WOMAN

By this point in your journey with this book, I hope you're ready to start integrating and embodying an entirely new frequency. One that's not only going to align you with the person that you're meant for, but with everything in life that was created just for you. Because that's really what union is all about: It's you, finding union with all that you are and with all that is.

One of the first steps in this process is becoming the chosen woman—one who reclaims her power on the deepest level, chooses herself in ways you have likely never done before (and ways no one else has ever done before), and aligns with the frequency of being chosen. Because "chosen" is a frequency.

I get this question from clients all the time: How do I know if I'm choosing myself? That's a really great question. Ultimately, the only way to know if you're choosing yourself is to actually know yourself. And that's what this chapter will explore: Knowing yourself so that you can finally choose yourself in the ways that you've been wanting a man to choose you.

So how does one get to know herself?

I remember being invited by one of my friends and her husband to Miami for the 10x Growth Con about a week after my divorce, and knowing it was something I had to do. I had recently started listening to Elena Cardone's podcast, and the intro was all about the event. My girlfriend said she was going and there were all these signs telling me I had to go. By signs I mean angel numbers everywhere.

So I pumped a bunch of milk, said goodbye to my baby for 5 days, and went to Miami. By myself. My first solo trip. Ever.

I arrived in Miami, got to my Airbnb, and realized I had chosen a terrible neighbourhood to stay in. It did not feel safe in any way, shape, or form. And I remember sitting in the Airbnb, thinking to myself that I didn't even want to leave the room. I was alone. I was devastated in a lot of ways. And I was faced with the reality that without my marriage and without my baby, I had no idea who I was.

Although from the outside, nobody would have ever known. With my disorganized attachment style, I had always tended to seem okay on the outside.

That was a pretty unsettling experience for people around me and a very lonely one for me, as I often felt very deeply misunderstood. Internally, there was so much pain, so much to process, but the outside world was not seeing that, and I was not even consciously feeling it. That wouldn't happen until years later, alone in an apartment, sobbing my eyes out endlessly, feeling like I could not breathe as I finally faced the pain that I had never been willing to face.

Attachment styles give us a way to understand ourselves and our healing. I don't always agree with them. They can all be healed. Your attachment style really just comes down to the egoic subpersonalities that were created through trauma in the early years that affected how you attached to your parents or caregivers. If you didn't have crazy trauma involving your mom or dad, you'll form secure attachments, generally. But if there were traumatic incidents, egoic sub-personalities would be created. Part of you that's afraid of abandonment, part of you that's afraid of intimacy, etc. But if you go to heal those, you become secure in your attachment.

Anxious attachment is characterized by fear of abandonment. Fear of losing the connection, fears of being alone. On the other hand, avoidant attachment is a desire for intimacy, but there's a fear of that closeness, a fear of a loss of self or engulfment. It often occurs due to parental enmeshment.

In reality, it's all avoidance. Two sides of the same coin. The anxious are chasing externally to get some sort of connection while they avoid the deep pain that they're feeling, the fear of abandonment, the fear of being alone, the fear that they're not enough. They're internally avoidant.

The avoidant has external *and* internal avoidance. This person avoids parts of themselves that they don't want to feel, while also avoiding people in their external reality. Once we can heal and feel these parts of ourselves, the avoidance goes away.

This is why I don't want my clients to label themselves. They put themselves in a prison of anxious attachment, and they have no motivation to heal on a deeper level.

It could take many years, but you can definitely heal your attachment style with the kind of work I do with clients through UNION.

Nowadays, though, I approach the feelings head-on and consciously. I regularly set a timer and just feel what I need to feel, no matter what it is or where I am. I am consistently tapped in and aligned with my heart, my soul, and my feelings, and I'm very proud of myself for how much I have healed my attachment style and for truly becoming secure.

That's after many years of living with a fearful avoidant or disorganized attachment style. This showed up not just in relationships but in my goals, in my business, and then those very deep fears of loss. It was confusing and messy, and I am finally in a secure place in my life and relationship. It is such a testament to the work I do with myself and with my clients.

At this time, my business was not really a business. I had been posting online consistently for about 8 months, and I was a personal trainer. But I had no idea what I wanted to do. I just knew that I wanted more. I was at a really deeply uncomfortable place in my life, a place where all of my trauma started to bubble up to the surface and catch up with me. I had come to a point where I had no choice but to truly change my life in pretty much every way.

I realized that I had been living a lie. That my marriage was a lie. That everything I'd built up until that point was a lie. I texted my two best friends at the time (whom I'd met at an entrepreneurial event called Pays to Be Brave in San Diego), just reaching out for a bit of a lifeline. I remember thinking, "What do I like? What do I like to do?"

I thought, "I like walking...Great, let me go for a walk. What else do I like? I like to eat. Perfect, let me go eat."

I started walking down the streets of Miami and found a really nice restaurant. I sat at the bar and ordered food I loved. I went home, went to bed, and the next morning, around 6 AM, my two best friends at the time surprised me by saying they were joining me for this 10x Growth Con experience.

This was how I started to get to know myself outside of the trauma. Outside of who my mom wanted me to be, outside of who I'd made myself be to feel worthy of marriage, outside of being a mom (even though that is an identity I so deeply love and am so grateful for).

I started to live my life in alignment with who I actually was.

Now here I am seven years later. Scaling the most incredible company, writing this book, working with women all over the world, helping them heal themselves, find themselves, and create the love and lives that they truly deserve.

Who are you outside of who you've been taught to be? Who are you outside of the relationships that you've had, outside of the current friendships that you have, outside of maybe your career or being a mom or whatever it is that you may have been attached to or what you've been living in?

Sometimes the life that we're in keeps us from seeing who we actually are.

This is actually one of the main reasons many women get scared of doing this deep work with me. They know that when we open up the hood to see what's going on underneath, they are going to have to make changes.

To be ignorant is one thing. But to be aware and to continue to self-abandon or neglect what it is that you now know to be true is betrayal of the deepest form. You're betraying yourself, what you know to be true, and what you actually need in order to feel happy, free, and at peace.

That can be scary. Changing our lives can be scary. Choosing ourselves can be scary.

Becoming the chosen woman first involves getting to know yourself.

So I want you to look around your room. Look around your house. Look at your clothes. Do you like how these things make you feel? Do they feel like the true you? Or do they feel like a safe version of you? The version of you that you have to be for the world?

I remember I had a client who was a real estate agent. She consistently believed she had to dress a certain way to make money. Sure, that could be true on some level. On a deeper level, that is absolutely not true.

On a deeper energetic level, the clients who are truly meant for you will find you when you are actually dressing and being your truest self.

It's so beautiful. I just recently saw her Facebook profile, where she's totally dressing like the spiritual hippie that she actually is, and is in a relationship with a beautiful man, and clearly so much happier than she's ever been. It makes me feel so excited for her and so proud of her for breaking out of those stories and limitations she's been living in to finally find union.

You need to become aware of how you're currently living and whether you might be in a state of self-abandonment, rejecting yourself out of fear that others will reject you, shrinking and minimizing yourself out of fear of being too much.

I did a photo shoot the other day, and I told my photographer I couldn't wait for fall because I have so many fur jackets. My stepdaughter always says I'm so extra, and I think, yes, I am. I am very extra, and I have no shame about it.

As silly as it may sound, that is you choosing yourself, not the you that will be anything other than yourself out of fear of what other people are going to think or say about you. At the end of the day, people are always going to judge you no matter what you do, so you might as well do what's going to make you happy.

At some point, you're going to be the talk of the town. I'd rather be the talk of the town knowing that I'm deeply fulfilled than the talk of the town knowing that I'm totally miserable because I'm completely out of alignment with who I want to be.

Choosing yourself is so much deeper than just going to the gym or choosing to eat healthier. You're going to have to choose parts of yourself that have likely been repressed and rejected your entire life.

It's in choosing these parts that you become what's called Self-sourced. You're no longer looking for external validation because you have all the validation that you need internally.

Look at the fur jackets. I don't need somebody to tell me if that was cool or not. I decided it was cool because it is cool for me.

When my son was about five, one of my favourite things was that he always wanted to see if things were "cool." He would constantly ask me, "Is this cool?" I would answer in the same way each time: "Do you think it's cool?"

I want him to be Self-sourced. I don't want him to go through the life I went through, where I was consistently at the mercy of everybody's judgment and rejection. That's not the life that any of us are meant to have. We are meant to *own* who we are at the core.

If I'm driving on the street and I see someone walking down the side of the road with a top hat, I'm like YES. YES. That is somebody who is free to just be themselves. That is magnetic.

Why? Because a magnet does two things: It draws objects in, and it pushes objects out. It attracts and repels.

That person with a top hat might be totally repelling a bunch of people who are like, "Oh my gosh, why is he wearing a top hat on Monday at 9 AM?" I have no idea why he is, but he doesn't care. To me, that is the vibe that we all need to be in. He will attract his people. Other people who wear top hats or do whatever on Monday morning, and he's going to repel all the people that don't.

Ultimately, it's not even that they're in judgment of him. They're in judgment of themselves. They would never dare do that, as, sadly for them, they're still at the mercy of everyone's thoughts and opinions about themselves and care more about what other people think than what they think. They are not truly free.

Which makes them the opposite of magnetic.

Become the chosen woman. Step into the chosen frequency, and into your magnetism, which is true feminine power, when you no longer care what's going on externally in the world and are so resolute in who it is that you are and what it is that you value and what it is that you want.

You become magnetic, you become the chosen woman when you decide that nothing outside of you is more important than your own internal love and your fulfillment.

Meaning, when you decide to no longer betray yourself to be chosen.

Chapter 16

THE CHASER, ORACLE & KING

I briefly considered using this chapter's title for the entire book because it beautifully describes the transformation this book is meant to guide you through. A transformation from chasing energy into, yes, the chosen woman, but also the oracle—the energy that calls a man into his king self.

Though you likely know by now, a review is appropriate at this point:

The chaser is a woman operating from wounded parts of herself—someone who avoids deeper aspects of herself, deeper pain she doesn't want to (or is unable to) feel. And so, unconsciously decides she would rather run away from not feeling good enough, unworthy, or undeserving, and towards a man in an attempt to have him choose her so that she will no longer need to feel the way that she so deeply doesn't want to feel.

The chaser is a wounded archetype of the feminine, and in my coaching work, I've outlined *Six Archetypes of Chasing*:

- The Performer (Identity Chasing – overdoing/performing)
- The Over-Giver (Behavioural Chasing – fixing, mothering, pouring)
- The Withholder (Energetic Chasing – pretending not to care, waiting, strategizing)

- The Anxious Heart (Emotional Chasing – spiralling, reassurance-seeking)
- The Illusionist (Spiritual Chasing – projecting fantasy, chasing potential)
- The Self-Abandoner/Collapser (Avoidant Chasing – shrinking, silencing, underdoing)

Ultimately, it doesn't matter which one you fall under. Each archetype stems from an ego or multiple ego subpersonalities of yours and can all manifest as certain dynamics in your external reality, such as a lack of commitment, a man being more in his feminine, passive energy, a man not rising and stepping up, a man only wanting something casual, a man ghosting you, etc.

Obviously, men are sovereign beings and are responsible for their own choices, or rather, should be. And you may be a lucky lady who is still in chasing energy that has a man showing up properly for you, and that is beautiful, and I'm happy for you. There are actually a lot of women who end up meeting a man who, through his love, ends up healing a lot of her own wounding, and I pray for that for every single person reading this.

However, much of the time, as you've seen in this book and as I've seen with my clients over my almost eight years of doing this work, the external masculine—the man—is responding to you, the feminine. And so when you are in chasing energy, he will likely respond differently than if you were to be healed, whole, and holy in the way you were intended to be.

Being chased by women actually ruins men. If you are chasing, he will be running. If you are emotionally unavailable, he will be, too.

But what we haven't talked about is the very important role the feminine plays in the masculine's life and in his becoming.

Through my studies with different teachers, I've concluded that the masculine can only be birthed, initiated, and become King through the feminine. I first heard of this idea from one of my beautiful teachers, Gillian Pothier, where I began to really tap into the creational codes of the feminine.

And so what we need to understand is that the masculine needs to see the truth of his own energy, embodiment, and seed to grasp who he is as a man and what and how he needs to grow.

Let's start with a metaphor, and then let's go into some real-life examples so that you can really understand what I'm saying. And this is one of the reasons it is so important that you commit and promise never to chase a man again. Because, as a collective, we are doing a disservice to men and the masculine at large by chasing them. Here's why:

The masculine and feminine are meant to work together as a system.

He provides. She receives.

She amplifies. And she gives back.

It's the whole "Give her a house, she'll make a home. Give her seed, she'll make a baby. Give her food, she'll make a meal." That's the feminine.

When you're chasing, it's the equivalent of you going to the grocery store, buying the food, and making the meal. It's the equivalent of you buying the house and making a home. It's the equivalent of you seeding yourself and making your own baby.

When you're chasing, you are not asking the masculine to give anything.

You are, just as we discussed in earlier chapters, overgiving, overfunctioning, moving towards him when he has made zero effort, given zero time, or given any indication that you are claimed, chosen, loved, or wanted.

If you make a promise and a commitment to stop chasing, and a man comes into your life who gives nothing (doesn't message you, doesn't plan a date, makes no effort whatsoever), then you say and do nothing because there is absolutely nothing for you to give back. He will then have no choice (if he really wants you) but to recognize that he may need to try a little harder to get your time, energy, affection, etc. He will need to step up if he wants a chance with you.

And this is good. This is right. This is how it's meant to be.

This is how men become inspired to become more.

This is how men are initiated into a King.

This is where they learn to let go of their breadcrumbing, nonchalance, and player ways in order to be chosen by their dream girl.

Let me say that one more time: To be chosen by his dream girl.

Not for you to wait for him to choose you.

For *you* to do the choosing.

This energy—you mirroring back his provision and his embodiment—is you being what I call the oracle.

You are being the woman that he needs. Not in a disempowered way, but in a way that allows him to finally see the truth of who he is and can become.

The oracle is the version of you that speaks her truth, and shares her wisdom and codes while no longer being afraid of upsetting him, or saying the wrong thing, or losing him.

Yes, the oracle is the oracle because she is no longer afraid to lose him. She would rather choose her Self, her truth, the deep wisdom emanating from her womb over the comfort of her wounded maiden.

This is the version of you that is in very high self-worth and understands the deeper nature of the relationship between masculine and feminine, and understands that her role is to give back, not to overfunction, overgive, perform, make a PowerPoint, put on a show, start a circus, or learn to do back flips for him to like her.

Why? She already likes herself.

She already has herself.

She wants him, and yes, she has space for him, and yes, in many ways, she needs him, but not in a wounded way where she needs him to fill a void or to make her feel worthy.

No.

Instead, she wants him in a healthy way: She recognizes that men and women both need each other. She knows that life is so much better when we are working together and have each other, and that ultimately you cannot be without the masculine just as he cannot be without you.

That is healthy interdependence, in contrast to the wounded need that stems from a sense of lack within your being and makes you dependent on his energy, actions, choices, and feelings towards you.

Now, where you might be falling short of embodying your Oracle energy is if you have not yet purified your channel. Meaning, you are filled with unprocessed trauma, trust wounds, betrayal, past heartbreak, abandonment, fears of being cheated on, etc.

All of these things cloud your perception. They prevent you from seeing the truth of situations as they affect both your unconscious mind's perception of the world and your neuroception, which stops you from living within your being and being truly embodied, and deters you from mirroring back the truth of *his* being.

This could present itself like this: You have a loving, loyal, consistent man, but because you haven't processed the past with your ex, who cheated on you, you consistently doubt his loyalty and question him, which, over time, erodes the relationship, as he is unable to see his love, loyalty, and true embodiment amplified within you.

He can't see you, nor can he see himself, because all that he can see is your past pain and trauma.

And this is where relationships tend to end, because they aren't serving the proper function of how the masculine and feminine are meant to operate together.

Circling back, chasing ruins a man because it gives him an illusion, a false sense of being this amazing, incredible king (yes, I put a small "k" for a reason) when he has not yet even gone through the hero's journey of truly becoming a man.

So when women throw themselves at men, they ruin them.

This allows men to live in ego and prevents them from seeing who they truly are.

This is why men who have women come to them so easily often don't know how to be in a relationship or how to maintain anything of substance. Because, again, they have a puffed-up ego created by a false mirroring coming from wounded feminine energy.

This creates what I call kings of the machine (or kings of the matrix, if you prefer).

They're not real kings.

They are unintegrated, often emotionally unavailable, and/or stuck in Peter Pan syndrome.

They're boys, as they have never been asked to step up as men and give to the feminine in order to receive back. They have just received without giving anything first.

So when you chase, you allow a man to remain a boy, and you prevent him from stepping into manhood.

This is a massive problem we are seeing worldwide.

And ladies, it is up to us to make a change and take action.

We are better than this.

We deserve more than Netflix and chill.

More than a man caught up in ego thinking he's so great when he is not even able to have a mature conversation without getting defensive, flipping it on you, etc.

And this would all stop if women stopped chasing.

Now, to be clear, I'm not victim-blaming women for the negative effects of this. Instead, I call us all to step back into our *true* power, not just as earthly women but as goddesses, priestesses, mystics, and birthers of our entire experience.

The only way you are going to become the oracle is for you to learn to receive, for you to learn to only give back, for you to heal your trauma, purify your vessel and mirror back a man's actions and provision so that he may choose to rise and become more for you, himself, his legacy, family, and the world at large.

Chapter 17

SHE WHO KNOWS HOW TO RECEIVE

This might be the biggest block you have to calling in the love of your life and your sacred union. Your inability to fully receive is one of the biggest reasons why you've been chasing. And being in a state of chasing energy is why you have not been able to receive. They work in tandem; it's a chicken-and-egg situation.

Imagine that you're running. You're chasing something. And I'm standing nearby, trying to give you a big bouquet. You won't be able to receive it, or even see it, because you're running, and that is completely masculine energy.

The only way to truly receive is to be in your feminine energy. And the only way to truly be in your feminine (as you may have figured out by now) is to stop doing.

This is easier said than done because when you stop doing, you start feeling. And that includes feeling all the things that you didn't want to feel. Hence, the running and chasing.

This is what receiving brings up. Imagine you're sitting on the couch, your man comes in, makes you dinner, brings you flowers, and you've done absolutely nothing.

For many, this can be extremely jarring for the nervous system and create a kind of cognitive dissonance.

Because if you don't believe that you are worthy as you are, then to receive like this, without having to overfunction, perform, prove, work your butt off, whatever it is that you've typically been doing, is not going to make sense to your system. Your body will reject it as it won't feel safe or normal.

This is why, a lot of the time, women will push away good love. When you're nitpicking your man, starting fights, and constantly creating issues with him over nothing, it's often a sign that you don't feel worthy of love, don't feel enough for love, and are unable to actually receive the love he's giving you.

Often in relationships, the man loves his woman deeply, but because she's unable to receive it, she can't see it. She doesn't feel it. And because she doesn't feel safe receiving, she tends to question everything that he's giving her:

- When is the other shoe gonna drop?
- What do I owe him?
- What does he expect from me?

If this sounds familiar to you, it's because your nervous system and your unconscious mind are trying to bring you back to homeostasis—trying to bring you back to your comfort zone, which currently might be that of not being loved, cherished, protected, provided for, etc.

So if things are going well with the guy you're seeing, but you haven't done the deep work to heal your wounds, you're going to create havoc in the relationship.

A lack of internal safety pushes us to create our own safety. And the biggest way that humans try to create safety for themselves is through control.

Controlling outcomes.

Controlling the narrative.

Controlling how he shows up, etc.

It's tough because controlling women get such a bad rap, and yet it stems from deep, deep, at times ancestral, generational parts of themselves. And ultimately, it stems from a tiny inner girl who has never felt safe to just *be*.

And then, when we add complex trauma into the mix, it can feel even more challenging to heal this pattern of attempting to create an illusion of safety through control. And chasing is one of the ways you try to take control, one of the ways you prevent yourself from actually receiving.

Now, the thing that I love about receiving is that it is intrinsically linked to worthiness.

The divine feminine is inherently worthy. She's different from the masculine, who has to go out and make a name for himself. The feminine vessel is literally directly created to receive, exactly as she is.

And so, learning to receive is one of the biggest reclamations of your femininity that you can experience—to decide that you are enough and worthy to receive as you are. Allowing yourself to have wants, needs, and desires, and allowing God or life or a man to fulfill them, is not only a reclamation but also a rebellion in a world that thrives on women feeling unworthy and not enough.

Building your capacity to receive is an essential part of healing the root of your feelings of unworthiness.

When you fall into hyper-independence, overgiving, overfunctioning, chasing, proving, and performing, you are inadvertently telling the world that you do not trust, believe, or feel worthy enough to know that the deep desires, wants, and needs within your heart, womb, and being will be fulfilled.

These patterns often stem from a deep, unresolved disappointment. Children do not have the tools to self-regulate or process really big, complicated emotions. And so they develop coping mechanisms.

As a little girl, there were likely things that you wanted—ice cream, a puppy, more alone time with your mom, playtime at the park with dad, a baby sibling—and over time, as these desires were not met, you likely began to feel intense wounds of disappointment. Maybe even betrayal. Which then turns into a lack of trust in life, in God, in the masculine.

And in an attempt to get rid of these feelings that you could not hold at that ripe, young age (and rightfully so), you decided to roll up your sleeves and make these things happen for yourself. You decided to meet your own needs.

And yes, obviously, we need to learn to meet our own needs, repair ourselves, self-regulate—all of the things. However, hyper-independence leaves little space for an actual relationship, so meeting our own needs must be balanced with receptivity.

None of the behaviours mentioned above (in which you are stepping into masculine energy and taking things into your own hands to make things happen) creates space for you to actually have your needs met.

You are allowed to want to have a relationship. You are allowed to want a man to show up for you and plan dates for you. You are allowed to trust that when you share deep desires of your heart, someone will gladly want to meet them.

Yes...

You are allowed to have your needs met.

You are.

You are not asking for too much.

You are not a burden.

You are not hard to love.

You are beautiful, and perfect, and lovable, and sweet, and kind, and worthy, and more than enough. Believe me when I say this, someone wants to love you, exactly as you are, for all that you are.

What has to happen now is that you need to learn to receive.

Receiving is a capacity, just as with anything and everything, regarding your unconscious mind, nervous system, and all things wanting to move out of your comfort zone into better things.

So if you are a woman who is hyper-independent, constantly in masculine energy, it will likely feel extremely uncomfortable if a man enters your life who is kind, consistent, loving, ready to pay your rent, give you a car, completely financially support you, or whatever it is he's showing up with that's abundant and generous and loving.

I'm giving money and financial provision as an example, but I also believe we live in an era in which many women are meant to be stewards of wealth, and that masculine provision goes far beyond material and financial provision.

But tangible examples are the simplest ones to help you understand the principles at work here.

So again, if you've been doing everything for yourself, and a man comes in and asks to take your car to the mechanic for you and handle that for you, it will likely feel extremely unsafe and very hard to receive.

But for the whole masculine-feminine system to work, you need to be able to receive the masculine.

As we'll discuss further in a future chapter, he needs to see the amplification of his provision.

Believe me, if a great man comes in and you are never able to receive his love, compliments, insights, opinions, and ideas, he won't feel the way that he's meant to feel. And ultimately, he won't be fulfilled in the relationship.

This is actually a very common reason many women don't move past the dating phase into commitment. They don't know how to receive when a man opens the door for them, pulls out a chair, or gives a compliment.

So if you want a long-lasting, beautiful relationship with a man, you need to build your capacity to receive.

That said, it's doubtful that a human being will be able to instantly shift from chasing-performing, hyper-independence, never being able to take help from anyone or never being able to simply say "thank you" when somebody compliments her—to the next day waking up a brand-new woman ready to receive all of the world's abundance and love and all that there is to offer.

It's rare. I mean, I would love for you to be able to just wake up, snap your fingers, rub a lamp, make a wish, and have this be your new reality. But generally speaking, when you have been hardwired to live a certain way for 20, 30, 40 years, you're going to have to shift the wiring slowly but surely.

So I want you to practice receiving.

When somebody compliments you, say thank you.

Don't say:

- "Oh, I'm not wearing makeup."
- "Oh, I didn't wash my hair."
- "Oh, this old thing? This has been in my closet for years."

You say, "Thank you."

You allow yourself to be filled by the experience.

Your womb is like a chalice. Your body is a vessel.

Imagine yourself receiving the compliment in your body and holding it.

Practice receiving.

Let your man take something off your plate.

If the guy you're seeing asks if you need help with anything, tell him what you need help with.

And all of this might be really uncomfortable, it might be really scary, because maybe nobody has ever shown up for you.

And because when we allow someone to help us, when we allow ourselves to receive, we come face-to-face with the fact that they may not want to meet our needs.

They might not want to help us.

And that fear right there is at the root of your being in masculine energy.

It is at the root of your avoidance of being in your feminine.

So, how would you feel if you asked the man you're seeing to help you hang a painting and he said no?

What would you feel rejected, unworthy, undeserving, disappointed, or angry?

Whatever that feeling is, it is tied to a memory.

And that memory needs to be processed.

It needs to be felt.

Remember, children don't have the tools to process big emotions.

So things get pushed down and repressed in your body.

And then those repressed feelings (and memories and parts) get mirrored outward in your external reality.

Feeling and processing your feelings and memories is the reclamation of your feminine energy, your emotional availability, and your ability to receive that which has always been your birthright.

Let this chapter and this book be the end of your survival mode and coping mechanisms to avoid the feelings you've been running from your entire life.

Chapter 18

FROM CHOSEN TO SACRED UNION

You made it. You're choosing yourself.

You stopped chasing.

You're in your feminine energy.

You're ready to receive. You're practicing it in little ways every day.

Now what?

How do you go from being chosen to then finding yourself in sacred union?

Sacred union is not just some basic relationship.

This is *the* relationship that you've been calling in. The one where you not only get to love, and learn to love, and learn to be loved, but where you get to grow, practice, and become the woman that you were always created to be.

Because yes, that is what sacred union is about.

It's about going deeper. Healing. So that we can rise higher together and ultimately tap into the highest energetics that we could tap into as human beings by merging masculine and feminine together in the flesh.

Internally, you have a feminine and masculine energy. That's your internal state.

Imagine the power you step into when your insides completely match your outsides. That is what union is about. And on a larger, collective level, sacred union is about ushering in and birthing a new frequency on Earth, together.

Let's look at what actually births life.

What creates manifestation?

It is masculine and feminine together that create life.

It is, in fact, the only way to make a baby.

And a baby is a manifestation and expression of life.

Even plants have both masculine and feminine poles.

We can't deny this. We can't escape it.

And so this new Earth that all of these spiritual teachers speak so much about is being birthed through every single one of us individually and through our divine unions.

We are restoring ancient codes to the planet that have been lost for a long time.

And I don't know that there's anything more beautiful than that.

What does this look like in practice?

For starters, get very clear about what you want.

Now, we already did a chapter about getting rid of your list, so what I mean is knowing you want a deep partnership.

Do you want to build an empire together?

Do you want to create a family?

Do you want to grow together?

Do you want to evolve together?

Get clear on what it is that you want because, believe me, there are men out in the world who, just like you, are looking for true partnership, true commitment.

He's looking for his woman in the flesh, and he will recognize you when he sees you.

So once you're really clear on this…

And once you know that you've been choosing yourself and showing up in the way that you want to, you've shifted your apartment around, you've made changes to your life, you've applied for new jobs, you've cut out toxic friendships, you've begun to choose yourself, you've restarted the gym routine. You're doing the things to choose yourself deeply...

You're going to open yourself up to love.

You're going to feel into the desires of your heart for true, genuine partnership.

Dating

You gotta decide whether you want to be on dating apps or not.

Personally, I think you're probably far too precious and gorgeous to be swiped left on a dating app without anyone even feeling your energy—but that is just my opinion. I also have a ton of clients who meet the men who become their husbands or life partners on dating apps.

It's not about right or wrong here. It's about alignment.

If you feel in your heart of hearts that you are aligned with being on a dating app, that is the true feminine desire. And it isn't laced with the fear that you'll never meet anyone, the fear that you're running out of time, or you not believing that you can meet anybody in real life. If it comes from a true feminine desire that's not stemming from any wounds, then please, by all means, go on the dating app because your man is likely there.

But if you're only on a dating app because you think you have to be…

You're only on a dating app because your friends told you you had to…

Because you have to move on from Brad, or Chad, or whoever…

Because you don't believe that people meet in real life anymore…

You need to delete that app right now.

Because that is not aligned.

And if you were to be truly emotionally available—which you are becoming—you know that deep down, you don't actually want to be on the dating app.

You feel resentful on the dating app.

And it's time for you to live in alignment with your truth versus living how you've been living, like the noncommittal fuckboy who can't seem to ever do right by you.

Yes babe.

When you were emotionally unavailable, you were the equivalent of an emotionally unavailable man who is never able to meet your needs.

So let's break that pattern.

Let's break that habit.

Tap into what you actually want and need.

And get rid of those dang apps, because you and I both know you can meet your man at the gas station tomorrow.

And what you need to do to meet him and call him in…

Is be open to actually meeting him.

You need to go outside.

You need to lift your eyes from the pavement when you're walking your dog and look at the human beings around you.

You need to spread your wings.

You need to go to the dog park.

You need to play pickleball.

You need to go to that art fair.

You need to go hiking with your girlfriends.

You need to meet people.

You need to be alive.

Believe me, there are forces at play far greater than you that are maneuvering the pieces around so that you and your person can come together.

Setting The Tone

Now, once you meet someone, I want you to understand that it's incredibly important for you to set the proper tone of the relationship.

What I mean is that the masculine and feminine systems need to be set.

If you start out chasing, planning, and doing, you set the dynamic up so you're in your masculine, and he's in his feminine.

And believe you me, if you set this tone, knowing that men (because they are more of the physical and spiritual nature than we are) are slower to move, slower to see you and process, and much more set in stone than we are...

If you're reading this and you're in a relationship, you could testify to all the other ladies reading that you started the relationship pushing and doing and planning has set you up for a lifetime of you being resentful and frustrated, because for some odd reason, your man just won't do these things.

It's because you set the tone of the relationship, with you in the masculine and him in the feminine.

This isn't to say it has to be this way all the time, but at some point, you'll have to re-polarize the relationship.

This is actually something we go deep on inside UNION, helping you reset the tone so that you can be in the feminine and he can be in the masculine.

And although the teachings are for seven days, it can take a lot longer than that for you to reset the entire dynamic.

So what you want to do is start with the proper energy with you in your feminine.

This doesn't mean you do nothing.

This doesn't mean that you never text him.

It doesn't mean you never pay for a date.

It means that you give back.

It means that you move from feminine desire.

It means you are being authentic rather than falling into old patterns of proving, performing, doing, chasing, hiding, shrinking, overgiving, overfunctioning, etc.

It means you show up big.

Full. Raw. And real.

You show up completely unbothered about whether he likes you.

Completely unafraid of being alone.

Completely unafraid of rejection, of him thinking you're weird or whatever it is.

You show up fully and completely.

When you have a desire to message him, if it's true feminine desire, you message.

When he's paid for two or three dates, and you're now going mini-golfing and want to give back to him, you do it.

Or if you want to make him pumpkin bread, do that.

Move from true feminine desire.

Not because you're trying to get him to choose you.

Not because you need him to want you to feel worthy.

Because that is just who you are.

You are a wild, fun-loving, charismatic, bright, funny, opinionated woman.

And you are finally willing and ready to show all sides of yourself to this big, beautiful man in front of you, who can't help but look in awe at you…and spend his life with you.

Yeah, I'm gonna get ahead of it here. He wants to spend his life with you.

So the way you go from choosing yourself to being in sacred union…

Is finally opening yourself up.

And closing the separation that you were creating by deciding that you were not yet ready to be loved.

Chapter 19

LIVING THE ORACLE PATH

Sacred union: It's so much more than just about love.

At the core of it, it's about you.

Now, although this book is about chasing, I can't not end with a chapter about union and living as the oracle, the truest and highest embodiment of yourself.

What you'll really find is that although you want a man, and although he's going to be absolutely amazing…

What you also really want and what you've even been looking for through him, is yourself.

Because what happens when you find the man is that you see an aspect of yourself that you can only be with him.

Although you can be aspects of yourself with your sisters and your girlfriends, you can only be certain aspects with your man.

And so, he unlocks a beautiful piece of you.

But it is only a piece.

And finding union is an inner journey.

It's about you finding union with all that *Is,* and all that was meant for you. This happens when you let yourself be this higher archetype of Oracle, and allow life to flow through your channel easily and effortlessly...

As you create and attract and birth and create and attract, over and over and over, living the most epic, beautiful, authentic, spiritual, incredible life filled with the presence of God.

Because that's really what it's all about.

So, on this journey from chasing to chosen, my hope and my prayer are that, in choosing yourself, you are finally in your creativity.

You are finally in your expression.

You are finally in your mission, your purpose, the holy work that only you are here to do.

And this can only be seen and found when we do the deep work to get to the core of who we really are. When we finally start to feel worthy and enough for our desires, for our dreams, for that which we are really meant for.

So often, when women come and work with me, they don't even know what they're truly here for. They've been taught through society, parents, other kids, and the school system that they are only capable of so much.

They are taught to be realistic.

They are taught to play it safe.

Things are possible...but that isn't meant for them.

And when you work with me, when you step into my world, you start to realize that you were sold a lie.

That you were a bird caught in a cage, completely unaware of what it is that's truly meant for you.

And when we heal, and we remove that veil, you start to see.

You start to dream.

You start to believe.

You start to think:

"Hey, maybe I can write a book."

"Maybe I can start doing my yoga teacher training."

"Maybe I don't have to stay in this career because staying in this career is perpetuating my wound of not being chosen…because I am not even choosing me."

This is an invitation to be a living, walking, breathing embodiment of the oracle, the goddess, the priestess. This is the woman who not only has the man you've been waiting for, but also is a woman for whom the world has been waiting: The original, organic blueprint of yourself.

JOURNAL PROMPTS

1. Who was I before the world taught me I needed to work for love?
2. What am I most passionate about that only I am here to do?
3. Which mission feels alive? What am I meant to fight for and live for?

AS WE PART...

I want you to pause for a moment.

Not to rush ahead.

Not to try to figure out what's next, as you've so often done for most of your life. But to sit here, settle in and acknowledge what has already changed.

What you have finally been able to see and face within yourself.

What's ready to shift, and never again be the same.

I want you to practice. Loving yourself. Being with yourself. Recognizing yourself.

You may not feel radically different every day. You might still have moments where old patterns rear their ugly heads, where you might still long for love, and feel an aching desire and wonder when it will be your turn.

But that doesn't mean you've failed.

It means you're human.

That you're feminine and a woman.

And that you are alive.

This book, this process, *From Chasing to Chosen,* isn't about "getting" the guy or no longer feeling things we don't want to feel. It's actually the opposite. It's about being so true. So real. So present. So fully aware of every waking moment of your life that you are no longer willing to close, run, pretend, rush, work, try or do anything outside of being completely and utterly intimate with every single aspect of yourself and every single aspect of your life.

It was never about the man.

It was about you.

Realizing that this is *your* life.

And that you are allowed to live. To take up space. To be in your uniqueness, differences, and natural essence.

And most importantly, that you are worthy of love. And that through these wounded parts of you and wounded coping mechanisms, you have been blocking off the flow of life from moving and emanating through you and as you.

To be chosen is to finally choose to be as you were created to be.

That choice changes everything.

From this place, relationships stop being hard.

They become invitations.

Spaces where two whole people meet.

Fully and truly.

And whether love arrives quickly or slowly, loudly or quietly, you're no longer waiting for it to validate you.

Because you are already living from the frequency of being chosen.

Carry this knowing with you.

Let it guide you.

Let it shape what—and who—you allow into your life.

You don't need to chase what is meant for you.

It will recognize you.

Meet you.

And it will stay.

GLOSSARY

Ayahuasca. A drink brewed from psychedelic plants used across various South American cultures, often in a ritual context.

Black Cat Archetype/Energy. A social media trend (2024-25) where women are instructed to act unbothered and independent to attract a partner. In the context of the book, this is viewed as a protection mechanism and an illusion of control and safety, ultimately laced with wounding, performance, and protective mechanisms, and is not genuine power.

Chasing. The subtle, unconscious, and somatic act of contorting, performing, acting, trying, and doing to achieve a deeply desired outcome, typically a man's choice or commitment. It is driven by fear, lack, control, and performance, and stems from a desire to be wanted as proof of self-worth/enoughness rather than a genuine desire for the man himself. (Note: Distinct from the queer community's definition of chasing/chaser, wherein cis straight men fetishize transgender women.)

Chasing Energy. The underlying energetic state of fear, lack, control, and performance that motivates chasing behaviour. It is the act of stepping out of one's natural, feminine beingness and into a state of strategy to get what is wanted.

Chosen. The ideal state or "frequency" is the opposite of chasing. It is the energy of knowing and embodying one's enoughness and power, where a person is no longer hiding, shrinking, or self-abandoning in an attempt to be chosen.

The Divine Feminine. The spiritual concept of reclaiming elements of femininity that our patriarchal society has deemed unimportant or 'soft'. The idea of the Divine Feminine is to see those aspects of ourselves as just as essential and godly as masculine traits.

Emotional Unavailability. Being completely disconnected from oneself, including one's own feelings and needs, is often characterized by being closed-hearted and out of alignment. This internal state then extends to others, resulting in emotional unavailability in relationships.

Energetics. The idea that our thoughts possess positive and negative energy, which can influence our external reality.

Feminine Power. Power that is authentic and does not come from control or performance. It comes from alignment, truth, and embodiment, and involves trusting one's softness, emotions, and intuition.

Karmic Path/Trauma Loops. A deep, dark, repeating relationship pattern where the feeling of "butterflies" is actually a sign of unconscious tendencies attempting to close out old trauma loops, rather than a sign of "Real Love."

Law of Divine Oneness. The idea that everything in the universe is connected via energetics.

Masculine Power. Power that is societally admired, rewarded, and often defined by external factors such as strength, status, and the ability to lead, provide, and protect.

Mother Wound. Deep, unresolved issues stemming from a lack of unconditional love or perceived inadequacy in one's relationship with one's mother (e.g., "Do better," "not enough"), which are then unconsciously perpetuated by choosing men who cannot fully accept the woman for who she truly is.

The Oracle. The version of you that speaks her truth, and shares her wisdom and codes, while no longer being afraid of upsetting him, or saying the wrong thing, or losing him. The oracle mirrors and reflects her partner rather than waiting to be chosen.

Sacred Union. The highest form of relationship that can be achieved from the "Chosen Frequency," after moving from the energy of being "Chosen."

The Self. Your goals, dreams, and purpose; all the things that make you, you.

Somatic. Working with the body, rather than the mind.

Real Love. A connection that has "nothing to do with butterflies" (which are often a sign of a deep, dark, karmic path). It is a meeting in the space between two whole humans who are ready to stand unwavering, entirely in their enoughness and power, no longer hiding or self-abandoning.

The Wound Beneath the Want. The deep, underlying emotional pain and insecurity (such as unworthiness, shame, and not feeling "good enough") that chasing attempts to escape or cover up. The man/relationship is never the true want; it is an attempt to fill the "gaping hole" that was meant only to be filled by one's Self and the love of God.

WORKS CITED

Brenner, Abigail. "The Inner Language of the Subconscious." Psychology Today, January 29, 2013. https://www.psychologytoday.com/us/blog/in-flux/201301/the-inner-language-of-the-subconscious.

Cherry, Kendra. "4 Attachment Styles in Relationships." Verywell Mind, November 17, 2025. https://www.verywellmind.com/attachment-styles-2795344.

Christler, Joan C, and Ingrid Johnston-Robledo. "Woman's Embodied Self: Feminist Perspectives on Identity and Image." American Psychological Association, 2018. https://psycnet.apa.org/record/2017-32522-000.

Dziedzic, Flannery. "The Law of Divine Oneness." Medium, May 11, 2020. https://medium.com/@FlanneryDz/the-law-of-divine-oneness-b160e2f5d64.

Elliott, Carolyn. *Existential Kink: Unmask your shadow and embrace your power.* Newburyport, MA: Weiser Books, 2020.

Morales, Jessica I. "The Heart's Electromagnetic Field Is Your Superpower." Psychology Today, November 29, 2020. https://www.psychologytoday.com/us/blog/building-the-habit-of-hero/202011/the-hearts-electromagnetic-field-is-your-superpower?msockid=0e6a70b6f3f46689275f6344f2e66762.

Nin, Anaïs. Seduction of the Minotaur. United States: John Colligan, 1961.

Strayed, Cheryl. *Wild: From Lost to Found on the Pacific Crest Trail.* New York: Alfred A. Knopf, 2019. https://www.cherylstrayed.com/wild_108676.htm.

The Shack. Canada: Lionsgate Films, 2017. https://www.youtube.com/watch?v=CL0yUbSS5Eg.

Thueson, Andie. "Why Men Need Space, Something You Need to Understand." Andie Thueson - Success Starts With Soul Purpose, September 25, 2025. https://andiethueson.com/why-men-need-space/.

ABOUT KELSEY GAUDREAULT

Kelsey Gaudreault is a relationship coach specializing in feminine polarity and the healing of inner fragmentation. Following a spiritual awakening and a divorce that dismantled her self-abandonment patterns, she rebuilt her identity from the inside out—and now teaches women how to do the same.

She is the founder of UNION, a body of work devoted to restoring feminine integrity, strengthening the inner masculine, and ending the cycle of chasing in love.

Kelsey's work challenges mainstream dating advice by addressing the root beneath overgiving and emotional collapse: Fragmentation. Her teachings guide women back to wholeness—not through performance, but through integration.

Kelsey is a devoted mother, a lover of faux-fur jackets, and a fierce advocate for living an unapologetic life of truth.

www.ingramcontent.com/pod-product-compliance
Ingram Content Group UK Ltd.
Pitfield, Milton Keynes, MK11 3LW, UK
UKHW062311290726
14090UKWH00018B/1009

9 781961 826205